Hard Questions About:

Jesus Christ

I0200341

By: Only A. Guy

Hard Questions About: Jesus Christ

Published by Only A. Guy Publishing

Cover Art and Editing By Whyte Lady Designs L.L.C.

www.onlyaguy.com
www.facebook.com/onlyaguy
www.twitter.com/onlyaguy1

ISBN 13: 978-0-9847382-1-2
ISBN: 0-9847382-1-2

Printed in the USA.

If you like this book here are some others coming out by this author you may find enjoyable as well as educational:

2011
HARD QUESTIONS ABOUT GOD
THE BOOK OF PRAYERS
READ THE BIBLE IN A YEAR

2012
HARD QUESTIONS ABOUT THE HOLY SPIRIT
HARD QUESTIONS ABOUT SALVATION
HARD QUESTIONS ABOUT HEAVEN AND HELL
HARD QUESTIONS ABOUT ANGELS AND DEMONS

2013
HARD QUESTIONS ABOUT THE END TIMES
HARD QUESTIONS ABOUT CHRISTIANITY
HARD QUESTIONS ABOUT CREATION
HARD QUESTIONS ABOUT HUMANITY

2014
HARD QUESTIONS ABOUT LIFE'S DECISIONS
HARD QUESTIONS ABOUT CULTS AND RELIGIONS
HARD QUESTIONS ABOUT FALSE DOCTRINE
HARD QUESTIONS ABOUT PRAYER
HARD QUESTIONS ABOUT SIN

1. Question: "Who is Jesus Christ?"

Who is Jesus Christ? Unlike the question "Does God exist?" very few people have questioned whether Jesus Christ existed. It is generally accepted that Jesus was truly a man who walked on the earth in Israel almost 2000 years ago. The debate begins when the subject of Jesus' full identity is discussed. Almost every major religion teaches that Jesus was a prophet, or a good teacher, or a godly man. The problem is the Bible tells us that Jesus was infinitely more than a prophet, a good teacher, or a godly man.

C.S. Lewis in his book Mere Christianity writes the following: "I am trying here to prevent anyone from saying the really foolish thing that people often say about Him [Jesus Christ]: 'I'm ready to accept Jesus as a great moral teacher, but I don't accept his claim to be God.' That is the one thing we must not say. A man who was merely a man and said the sort of things Jesus said would not be a great moral teacher. He would either be a lunatic -- on a level with a man who says he is a poached egg -- or else he would be the Devil of Hell. You must make your choice. Either this man was, and is, the Son of God, or else a madman or something worse.... You can shut him up for fool, you can spit at him and kill him as a demon; or you can fall at his feet and call him Lord and God. But let us not come up with any patronizing nonsense about his being a great human teacher. He has not left that option open to us. He did not intend to."

So, who did Jesus claim to be? Who does the Bible say He was? First, let's look at Jesus' words in *John 10:30, "I and the Father are one."* At first glance, this might not seem to be a claim to be God. However, look at the Jews' reaction to His statement, *"We are not stoning you for any of these, replied the Jews, but for blasphemy, because you, a mere man, claim to be God" (John 10:33)*. The Jews understood Jesus' statement to be a claim to be God. In the following verses, Jesus never corrects the Jews by saying, "I did not claim to be God." That indicates Jesus was truly saying He was God by declaring, *"I and the Father are one" (John 10:30)*. John 8:58 is another example. Jesus proclaimed, *"I tell you the truth, Jesus answered, before Abraham was born, I am!"* Again, in response, the Jews take up stones in an attempt to stone Jesus *(John 8:59)*. Jesus announcing His identity as "I am" is a direct application of the Old Testament name for God *(Exodus 3:14)*. Why would the Jews again want to stone Jesus if He hadn't said something they believed to be blasphemous, namely, a claim to be God?

John 1:1 says that *"the Word was God." John 1:14* says that *"the Word became flesh."* This clearly indicates that Jesus is God in the flesh. Thomas the disciple declared to Jesus, *"My Lord and my God" (John 20:28).* Jesus does not correct him. The Apostle Paul describes Him as, *"...our great God and Savior, Jesus Christ" (Titus 2:13).* The Apostle Peter says the same, *"...our God and Savior Jesus Christ" (2 Peter 1:1).* God the Father is witness of Jesus' full identity as well, *"But about the Son he says, "Your throne, O God, will last forever and ever, and righteousness will be the scepter of your kingdom."* Old Testament prophecies of Christ announce His deity, *"For to us a child is born, to us a son is given, and the government will be on his shoulders. And he will be called Wonderful Counselor, Mighty God, Everlasting Father, Prince of Peace."*

So, as C.S. Lewis argued, believing Jesus to be a good teacher is not an option. Jesus clearly and undeniably claimed to be God. If He is not God, then He is a liar, and therefore not a prophet, good teacher, or godly man. In attempts to explain the words of Jesus away, modern "scholars" claim the "true historical Jesus" did not say many of the things the Bible attributes to Him. Who are we to argue with God's Word concerning what Jesus did or did not say? How can a "scholar" two-thousand years removed from Jesus have better insight into what Jesus did or did not say than those who lived with, served with, and were taught by Jesus Himself *(John 14:26)*?

Why is the question over Jesus' true identity so important? Why does it matter whether or not Jesus is God? The most important reason that Jesus has to be God is that if He is not God, His death would not have been sufficient to pay the penalty for the sins of the whole world *(1 John 2:2)*. Only God could pay such an infinite penalty *(Romans 5:8; 2 Corinthians 5:21)*. Jesus had to be God so that He could pay our debt. Jesus had to be man so He could die. Salvation is available only through faith in Jesus Christ! Jesus' deity is why He is the only way of salvation. Jesus' deity is why He proclaimed, *"I am the Way and the Truth and the Life. No one comes to the Father except through me" (John 14:6).*

2. Question: "Did Jesus really exist? Is there any historical evidence of Jesus Christ?"

Typically when this question is asked, the person asking qualifies the question with "outside of the Bible." We do not grant this idea that the Bible cannot be considered a source of evidence for the existence of Jesus. The New Testament contains hundreds of references to Jesus Christ. There are those who date the writing of the Gospels in the second century A.D., 100+ years after Jesus' death. Even if this were the case (which we strongly dispute), in terms of ancient evidences, writings less than 200 years after events took place are considered very reliable evidences. Further, the vast majority of scholars (Christian and non-Christian) will grant that the Epistles of Paul (at least some of them) were in fact written by Paul in the middle of the first century A.D., less than 40 years after Jesus' death. In terms of ancient manuscript evidence, this is extraordinarily strong proof of the existence of a man named Jesus in Israel in the early first century A.D.

It is also important to recognize that in 70 A.D., the Romans invaded and destroyed Jerusalem and most of Israel, slaughtering its inhabitants. Entire cities were literally burned to the ground! We should not be surprised, then, if much evidence of Jesus' existence was destroyed. Many of the eye-witnesses of Jesus would have been killed. These facts likely limited the amount of surviving eyewitness testimony of Jesus.

Considering the fact that Jesus' ministry was largely confined to a relatively unimportant backwater area in a small corner of the Roman Empire, a surprising amount of information about Jesus can be drawn from secular historical sources. Some of the more important historical evidences of Jesus include the following:

The first-century Roman Tacitus, who is considered one of the more accurate historians of the ancient world, mentioned superstitious "Christians " ("named after Christus" which is Latin for Christ), who suffered under Pontius Pilate during the reign of Tiberius. Suetonius, chief secretary to Emperor Hadrian, wrote that there was a man named Chrestus (or Christ) who lived during the first century (Annals 15.44).

Flavius Josephus is the most famous Jewish historian. In his Antiquities he refers to James, "the brother of Jesus, who was called Christ." There is a controversial verse (18:3) that says, "Now there was about this time Jesus, a wise man, if it be lawful to call him a man. For he was one who wrought surprising feats. . . . He was [the] Christ . . . he appeared to them alive again the third day, as the divine prophets had foretold these and ten thousand other wonderful things concerning him." One version reads, "At this time there was a wise man named Jesus. His conduct was good and [he] was known to be virtuous. And many people from among the Jews and the other nations became his disciples. Pilate condemned him to be crucified and to die. But those who became his disciples did not abandon his discipleship. They reported that he had appeared to them three days after his crucifixion, and that he was alive; accordingly he was perhaps the Messiah, concerning whom the prophets have recounted wonders."

Julius Africanus quotes the historian Thallus in a discussion of the darkness which followed the crucifixion of Christ (Extant Writings, 18).

Pliny the Younger, in Letters 10:96, recorded early Christian worship practices including the fact that Christians worshiped Jesus as God and were very ethical, and includes a reference to the love feast and Lord's Supper.

The Babylonian Talmud (Sanhedrin 43a) confirms Jesus' crucifixion on the eve of Passover, and the accusations against Christ of practicing sorcery and encouraging Jewish apostasy.

Lucian of Samosata was a second-century Greek writer who admits that Jesus was worshiped by Christians, introduced new teachings, and was crucified for them. He said that Jesus' teachings included the brotherhood of believers, the importance of conversion, and the importance of denying other gods. Christians lived according to Jesus' laws, believed themselves immortal, and were characterized by contempt for death, voluntary self-devotion, and renunciation of material goods.

Mara Bar-Serapion confirms that Jesus was thought to be a wise and virtuous man, was considered by many to be the king of Israel, was put to death by the Jews, and lived on in the teachings of his followers.

Then we have all the Gnostic writings (The Gospel of Truth, The Apocryphon of John, The Gospel of Thomas, The Treatise on Resurrection, etc.) that all mention Jesus.

In fact, we can almost reconstruct the gospel just from early non-Christian sources: Jesus was called the Christ (Josephus), did "magic," led Israel into new teachings, and was hanged on Passover for them (Babylonian Talmud) in Judea (Tacitus), but claimed to be God and would return (Eliezar), which his followers believed - worshipping Him as God (Pliny the Younger).

In conclusion, there is overwhelming evidence for the existence of Jesus Christ, both in secular and Biblical history. Perhaps the greatest evidence that Jesus did exist is the fact that literally thousands of Christians in the first century A.D., including the 12 apostles, were willing to give their lives as martyrs for Jesus Christ. People will die for what they believe to be true, but no one will die for what they know to be a lie.

$$\infty$$

3. Question: "Why should I believe in Christ's resurrection?"

It is a fairly well-established fact that Jesus Christ was publicly executed in Judea in the 1st Century A.D., under Pontius Pilate, by means of crucifixion, at the behest of the Jewish Sanhedrin. The non-Christian historical accounts of Flavius Josephus, Cornelius Tacitus, Lucian of Samosata, Maimonides and even the Jewish Sanhedrin corroborate the early Christian eyewitness accounts of these important historical aspects of the death of Jesus Christ.

As for His resurrection, there are several lines of evidence which make for a compelling case. The late jurisprudential prodigy and international statesman Sir Lionel Luckhoo (of The Guinness Book of World Records fame for his unprecedented 245 consecutive defense murder trial acquittals) epitomized Christian enthusiasm and confidence in the strength of the case for the resurrection when he wrote, "I have spent more than 42 years as a defense trial lawyer appearing in many parts of the world and am still in active practice. I have been fortunate to secure a number of successes in jury trials and I say unequivocally the evidence for the Resurrection of Jesus Christ is so overwhelming that it compels acceptance by proof which leaves absolutely no room for doubt."

The secular community's response to the same evidence has been predictably apathetic in accordance with their steadfast commitment to methodological naturalism. For those unfamiliar with the term, methodological naturalism is the human endeavor of explaining everything in terms of natural causes and natural causes only. If an alleged historical event defies natural explanation (e.g., a miraculous resurrection), secular scholars generally treat it with overwhelming skepticism, regardless of the evidence, no matter how favorable and compelling it may be.

In our view, such an unwavering allegiance to natural causes regardless of substantive evidence to the contrary is not conducive to an impartial (and therefore adequate) investigation of the evidence. We agree with Dr. Wernher von Braun and numerous others who still believe that forcing a popular philosophical predisposition upon the evidence hinders objectivity. Or in the words of Dr. von Braun, "To be forced to believe only one conclusion... would violate the very objectivity of science itself."

Having said that, let us now examine the several lines of evidence which favor of the resurrection.

A. The First Line of Evidence for Christ's Resurrection

To begin with, we have demonstrably sincere eyewitness testimony. Early Christian apologists cited hundreds of eyewitnesses, some of whom documented their own alleged experiences. Many of these eyewitnesses willfully and resolutely endured prolonged torture and death rather than repudiate their testimony. This fact attests to their sincerity, ruling out deception on their part. According to the historical record (*The Book of Acts 4:1-17*; Pliny's Letters to Trajan X, 96, etc) most Christians could end their suffering simply by renouncing the faith. Instead, it seems that most opted to endure the suffering and proclaim Christ's resurrection unto death. Granted, while martyrdom is remarkable, it is not necessarily compelling. It does not validate a belief so much as it authenticates a believer (by demonstrating his or her sincerity in a tangible way). What makes the earliest Christian martyrs remarkable is that they knew whether or not what they were professing was true. They either saw Jesus Christ alive-and-well after His death or they did not. This is extraordinary. If it was all just a lie, why would so many perpetuate it given their circumstances? Why would they all

6

knowingly cling to such an unprofitable lie in the face of persecution, imprisonment, torture, and death? While the September 11, 2001, suicide hijackers undoubtedly believed what they professed (as evidenced by their willingness to die for it), they could not and did not know if it was true. They put their faith in traditions passed down to them over many generations. In contrast, the early Christian martyrs were the first generation. Either they saw what they claimed to see, or they did not. Among the most illustrious of the professed eyewitnesses were the Apostles. They collectively underwent an undeniable change following the alleged post-resurrection appearances of Christ. Immediately following His crucifixion, they hid in fear for their lives. Following the resurrection they took to the streets, boldly proclaiming the resurrection despite intensifying persecution. What accounts for their sudden and dramatic change? It certainly was not financial gain. The Apostles gave up everything they had to preach the resurrection, including their lives.

B. Second Line of Evidence for Christ's Resurrection

A second line of evidence concerns the conversion of certain key skeptics, most notably Paul and James. Paul was of his own admission a violent persecutor of the early Church. After what he described as an encounter with the resurrected Christ, Paul underwent an immediate and drastic change from a vicious persecutor of the Church to one of its most prolific and selfless defenders. Like many early Christians, Paul suffered impoverishment, persecution, beatings, imprisonment, and execution for his steadfast commitment to Christ's resurrection. James was skeptical, though not as hostile as Paul. A purported post-resurrection encounter with Christ turned him into an inimitable believer, a leader of the Church in Jerusalem. We still have what scholars generally accept to be one of his letters to the early Church. Like Paul, James willingly suffered and died for his testimony, a fact which attests to the sincerity of his belief (see *The Book of Acts* and Josephus' Antiquities of the Jews XX, ix, 1).

C. The Third and Fourth Lines of Evidence for Christ's Resurrection

A third line and fourth line of evidence concern enemy attestation to the empty tomb and the fact that faith in the resurrection took root in Jerusalem. Jesus was publicly executed and buried in Jerusalem. It would have been impossible for faith in His resurrection to take root in Jerusalem while His body was still in the tomb where the Sanhedrin could exhume it, put it on public display, and thereby expose the hoax. Instead, the Sanhedrin accused the disciples of stealing the body, apparently in an effort to explain its disappearance (and therefore an empty tomb). How do we explain the fact of the empty tomb? Here are the three most common explanations. First, the disciples stole the body. If this were the case, they would have known the resurrection was a hoax. They would not therefore have been so willing to suffer and die for it. (See the first line of evidence concerning demonstrably sincere eyewitness testimony.) All of the professed eyewitnesses would have known that they hadn't really seen Christ and were therefore lying. With so many conspirators, surely someone would have confessed, if not to end his own suffering then at least to end the suffering of his friends and family. The first generation of Christians were absolutely brutalized, especially following the conflagration in Rome in A.D. 64 (a fire which Nero allegedly ordered to make room for the expansion of his palace, but which he blamed on the Christians in Rome in an effort to exculpate himself). As the Roman historian Cornelius Tacitus recounted in his Annals of Imperial Rome (published just a generation after the fire). "Nero fastened the guilt and inflicted the most exquisite tortures on a class hated for their abominations, called Christians by the populace. Christus, from whom the name had its origin, suffered the extreme penalty during the reign of Tiberius at the hands of one of our procurators, Pontius Pilatus, and a most mischievous superstition, thus checked for the moment, again broke out not only in Judaea, the first source of the evil, but even in Rome, where all things hideous and shameful from every part of the world find their centre and become popular. Accordingly, an arrest was first made of all who pleaded guilty; then, upon their information, an immense multitude was convicted, not so much of the crime of firing the city, as of hatred against mankind. Mockery of every sort was added to their deaths. Covered with the skins of beasts, they were torn by dogs and perished, or were nailed to crosses, or were doomed to the flames and burnt, to serve as a nightly illumination, when daylight had expired." (Annals, XV, 44) Nero illuminated his garden parties with Christians whom he burnt alive. Surely someone would have confessed the truth under the threat of such terrible pain. The fact is, however, we have no record of any early Christian denouncing the faith to end his suffering. Instead, we have multiple accounts of post-resurrection appearances and hundreds of eyewitnesses willing to suffer and die for it. If the disciples didn't steal the body, how else do we explain the empty tomb? Some have suggested that Christ faked His death and later escaped from the tomb. This is patently absurd. According to the eyewitness testimony, Christ was beaten, tortured, lacerated, and stabbed. He suffered internal damage, massive blood loss, asphyxiation, and a spear through His heart. There is no good reason to believe that Jesus Christ (or any other man for that matter) could survive such an ordeal, fake His death, sit in a tomb for three days and nights without medical attention, food or water, remove the massive stone which sealed His tomb, escape undetected (without leaving behind a trail of blood), convince hundreds of eyewitnesses that He was resurrected from the death and in good health, and then disappear without a trace. Such a notion is ridiculous.

D. The Fifth Line of Evidence for Christ's Resurrection
Finally, a fifth line of evidence concerns a peculiarity of the eyewitness testimony. In all of the major resurrection narratives, women are credited as the first and primary eyewitnesses. This would be an odd invention since in both the ancient Jewish and Roman cultures women were severely disesteemed. Their testimony was regarded as insubstantial and dismissible. Given this fact, it is highly unlikely that any perpetrators of a hoax in 1st Century Judea would elect women to be their primary witnesses. Of all the male disciples who claimed to see Jesus resurrected, if they all were lying and the resurrection was a scam, why did they pick the most ill-perceived, distrusted witnesses they could find? Dr. William Lane Craig explains, "When you understand the role of women in first-century Jewish society, what's really extraordinary is that this empty tomb story should feature women as the discoverers of the empty tomb in the first place. Women were on a very low rung of the social ladder in first-century Palestine. There are old rabbinical sayings that said, 'Let the words of Law be burned rather than delivered to women' and 'blessed is he whose children are male, but woe to him whose children are female.' Women's testimony was regarded as so worthless that they weren't even allowed to serve as legal witnesses in a Jewish court of Law. In light of this, it's absolutely remarkable that the chief witnesses to the empty tomb are these women... Any later legendary account would have certainly portrayed male disciples as discovering the

tomb - Peter or John, for example. The fact that women are the first witnesses to the empty tomb is most plausibly explained by the reality that - like it or not - they were the discoverers of the empty tomb! This shows that the Gospel writers faithfully recorded what happened, even if it was embarrassing. This bespeaks the historicity of this tradition rather than its legendary status." (Dr. William Lane Craig, quoted by Lee Strobel, The Case For Christ, Grand Rapids: Zondervan, 1998, p. 293)

E. In Summary

These lines of evidence: the demonstrable sincerity of the eyewitnesses (and in the Apostles' case, compelling, inexplicable change), the conversion and demonstrable sincerity of key antagonists- and skeptics-turned-martyrs, the fact of the empty tomb, enemy attestation to the empty tomb, the fact that all of this took place in Jerusalem where faith in the resurrection began and thrived, the testimony of the women, the significance of such testimony given the historical context; all of these strongly attest to the historicity of the resurrection. We encourage our readers to thoughtfully consider these evidences. What do they suggest to you? Having pondered them ourselves, we resolutely affirm Sir Lionel's declaration:

"The evidence for the Resurrection of Jesus Christ is so overwhelming that it compels acceptance by proof which leaves absolutely no room for doubt."

⊂×

4. Question: "Is the resurrection of Jesus Christ true?"

Scripture presents conclusive evidence that Jesus Christ was in fact resurrected from the dead. Christ's resurrection is recorded in *Matthew 28:1-20; Mark 16:1-20; Luke 24:1-53;* and *John 20:1-21:25.* The resurrected Christ also appeared in the *Book of Acts (Acts 1:1-11).* From these passages you can gain several "proofs" of Christ's resurrection. First, look at the dramatic change in the disciples. They went from scared and hiding in a room, to courageous and sharing the Gospel throughout the world. What else could explain this dramatic change other than the risen Christ appearing to them?

Second, look at the life of the Apostle Paul. What changed him from being a persecutor of the church into an apostle for the church? It was when the risen Christ appeared to him on the road to Damascus (*Acts 9:1-6*). Third, another convincing "proof" is the empty tomb. If Christ were not raised, then where is His body? The disciples and others saw the tomb where He was buried. When they returned, His body was not there. Angels declared that He had been raised from the dead as He had promised (*Matthew 28:5-7*). Fourth, additional evidence of His resurrection is the many people He appeared to (*Matthew 28:5, 9, 16 & 17; Mark 16:9; Luke 24:13-35; John 20:19, 24, 26-29; 21:1-14; Acts 1:6-8; 1 Corinthians 15:5-7*).

Another key truth to why the resurrection of Jesus must be true is the great amount of weight the Apostles gave to Jesus' resurrection. A key passage on Christ's resurrection is *1 Corinthians 15*. In this chapter, the Apostle Paul explains why it is crucial to understand and believe in Christ's resurrection. The resurrection is important for the following reasons:

A. If Christ was not raised from the dead, believers will not be either (*1 Corinthians 15:12-15*).

B. If Christ was not raised from the dead, His sacrifice for sin was not sufficient (*1 Corinthians 15:16-19*). Jesus' resurrection proved that His death was accepted by God as the atonement for our sins. If He had simply died and stayed dead, that would indicate His sacrifice was not sufficient. As a result, believers would not be forgiven for their sins, and they would still remain dead after they die (*1 Corinthians 15:16-19*) – there would be no such thing as eternal life (*John 3:16*). *"But now Christ has been raised from the dead, the first fruits of those who are asleep"* (*1 Corinthians 15:20 NAS*). Christ has been raised from the dead – He is the first fruits of our resurrection.

C. All those who believe in Him will be raised to eternal life just as He was (*1 Corinthians 15:20-23*). *1 Corinthians 15* goes on to describe how Christ's resurrection proves His victory over sin, and provides us the power to live victoriously over sin (*1*

Corinthians 15:24-34).

D. It describes the glorious nature of the resurrection body we will receive (*1 Corinthians 15:35-49*).

E. It proclaims that as a result of Christ's resurrection, all who believe in Him have ultimate victory over death (*1 Corinthians 15:50-58*). What a glorious truth the resurrection of Christ is! *"Therefore, my beloved brethren, be steadfast, immovable, always abounding in the work of the Lord, knowing that your toil is not in vain in the Lord" (1 Corinthians 15:58).*

According to the Bible, the resurrection of Jesus Christ is most definitely true. The Bible records Christ's resurrection, records that it was eye-witnessed by over 400 people, and proceeds to build crucial Christian doctrine on the historical fact of Jesus' resurrection.

$\propto$

5. Question: "What is the Jesus Family Tomb? Has the lost tomb of Jesus Christ been discovered?"

In 1980, in Talpiot (a suburb of Jerusalem), Israel, a construction crew unearthed an ancient tomb. Inside the tomb was discovered ten (or nine) ossuaries (burial bone boxes). Inscribed on these bone boxes were names. The discovery of the ossuaries was not unusual, as thousands of ancient ossuaries have been discovered in ancient tombs in and around Jerusalem. What was somewhat unusual were the names that were inscribed on the ossuaries: Jesus son of Joseph, Maria, Mariamene, Matthew, Judas son of Jesus, and Jose (likely an abbreviation of Joseph). The similarities of these names to the biblical Jesus and His family have led TV director Simcha Jacobovici and movie producer James Cameron to produce "The Jesus Family Tomb" in book form and "The Lost Tomb of Jesus" as a movie / documentary. Jacobovici and Cameron are making the claims that the Jesus Family Tomb is indeed the family burial place of Jesus and His family, and that the presence of Jesus' bones disproves His resurrection. Is there any validity to the claims of the Jesus Family Tomb?

First, before we examine the question biblically, it is important to understand that no influential archaeologist has come forward in agreement with the Jesus Family Tomb project. The curator for anthropology and archeology at the Rockefeller Museum in Jerusalem from 1972 to 1997, Joe Zias, states that the project "makes a mockery of the archaeological profession." Second, there is evidence that the tomb had been disturbed and vandalized. It cannot be verified what was, or what was not, vandalized or stolen. On an archaeological basis alone, there is serious reason to doubt the authenticity of the Jesus Family Tomb project.

Historically and culturally speaking, there is further reasoning to reject the ideas of the Jesus Family Tomb project. The names "Jesus, Maria, Matthew, Judas, and Joseph" were all very common names in 1st century Israel. Some cultural historians estimate that as many as 25% of 1st century Jewish women were named Mary (Miriam). The New Testament confirms this by mentioning six different women named Mary, including three who were prominent in Jesus' life (Jesus' mother, Mary Magdalene, and Mary of Bethany). It would not be uncommon for a 1st century Jewish family to have the names Jesus (Yeshua), Mary (Miriam), Joseph, and Judas (Judah) – as all were very popular Jewish names (due to their background in the Hebrew Scriptures).

Biblically speaking, there are numerous reasons to reject the idea of the Jesus Family Tomb. First, the New Testament consistently states that Jesus' family was from Nazareth (*Matthew 2:13; Luke 2:4, 39, 51; John 1:45 & 46*). If Jesus' family had a tomb, it would have very likely been in Nazareth. Second, the Bible describes Jesus and his adopted father Joseph as carpenters (*Matthew 13:55; Mark 6:3*), likely making them financially poor and of a lower social status. The tomb discovered in Talpiot is the tomb of a wealthy family. Third, the New Testament states that Jesus' body was buried in a tomb that belonged to Joseph of Arimathea, and that there were witnesses as to where Jesus was buried (*Matthew 27:57-61; Mark 15:43-47; Luke 23:50-54; John 19:38-42*).

The "Lost Tomb of Jesus" documentary advocates the concept that Jesus' disciples stole His body from the tomb, and then buried it in His family tomb. If the disciples were going to steal Jesus' body in an attempt to argue for a resurrection, why would they then bury Jesus' body in His own family's tomb, and even inscribe Jesus' name on His ossuary? That does not make any sense whatsoever. If the disciples wanted to fake a resurrection, the last thing they would do would be to bury Jesus in His family tomb (which other people could easily examine) and write Jesus' name on His ossuary (providing undeniable evidence that Jesus was not resurrected). Without even considering the evidence for the resurrection of Jesus, the New Testament account paints an entirely different account of Jesus, His family, and His burial.

Now, let's get to the crux of the matter. The true motivation of the Jesus Family Tomb project is to deny the resurrection of Jesus Christ. The subtitle of the book is given as "The Discovery, the Investigation, and the Evidence That Could Change History." Cameron, Jacobovici, and co-author Pellegrino have a clear agenda. They do not believe that Jesus was the Messiah, that Jesus was God-incarnate, or that Jesus was resurrected after His crucifixion. The discovery of the "Jesus Family Tomb" is simply a convenient basis for their argument, due to the similarities of the names on the ossuaries to the names of Jesus and His family. If it could be proven that the "Jesus Family Tomb" was indeed the tomb of the biblical Jesus of Nazareth and His family, the resurrection would be disproven, thus destroying the very foundation of the Christian faith (see *1 Corinthians chapter 15*).

None of the suppositions of the Jesus Family Tomb project can be proven. In fact, the archaeological community is nearly unanimous in condemning the Jesus Family Tomb as a hoax, with no basis in history or archaeology. There is every reason to doubt the claims of the Jesus Family Tomb – archaeologically, historically, and biblically. The Christian faith has nothing to fear from honest and scientific archaeology.

 ⊂✕

6. Question: "What is Christology?"

The word "Christology" comes from two Greek words meaning "Christ/Messiah" and "word" - which combine to mean "the study of Christ." Christology is the study of the Person and work of Jesus Christ. There are numerous important questions that Christology answers:

Who is Jesus Christ? Almost every major religion teaches that Jesus was a prophet, or a good teacher, or a godly man. The problem is, the Bible tells us that Jesus was infinitely more than a prophet, a good teacher, or a godly man.

Is Jesus God? Did Jesus ever claim to be God? Although Jesus never uttered the words "I am God," He made many other statements that can't be properly interpreted to mean anything else.

What is the hypostatic union? How can Jesus be both God and man at the same time? The Bible teaches that Jesus is both fully human and fully divine, that there is no mixture or dilution of either nature, and that He is one united Person, forever.

Why is the virgin birth so important? The virgin birth is a crucial biblical doctrine because it accounts for the circumvention of the transmission of the sin nature and allowed the eternal God to become a perfect man.

What does it mean that Jesus is the Son of God? Jesus is not God's Son in the sense of how we think of a father/son relationship. God did not get married and have a son. Jesus is God's Son in the sense that He is God made manifest in human form (*John 1:1, 14*).

A Biblical understanding of Jesus Christ is crucial to our salvation. Many cults and world religions claim to believe in Jesus Christ. The problem is that they do not believe in the Jesus Christ presented in the Bible. That is why Christology is so important. It helps us to understand the significance of the deity of Christ. It demonstrates why Jesus is the atoning sacrifice for our sins. Christology teaches us that Jesus had to be man so that He could die - and had to be God so that His death would pay for our sins. It is perhaps the most important area of theology. Without a proper understanding of who Jesus Christ is and what He accomplished, all other areas of theology will be errant as well.

An in-depth study of Christology has incredible personal impact on the believer's daily life. As we delve into the heart of Jesus, we begin to grasp the amazing concept that He, being fully Man and fully God, loves each of us with a never-ending love the extent of which is hard for us to imagine. The various titles and names of Christ in the Scriptures give insight into who He is and how He relates to us. He is our

Good Shepherd, leading, protecting and caring for us as one of His own (*John 10:11,14*); He is the Light of the world, illuminating our pathway through a sometimes dark and uncertain world (*John 8:12*); He is the Prince of Peace (*Isaiah 9:6*), bringing tranquility into our tumultuous lives; and He is our Rock (*1 Corinthians 10:4*), the immovable and secure base who we can trust to keep us safe and secure in Him.

$$\propto$$

7. Question: "Is the movie "The Passion of the Christ" Biblically accurate?"

The movie "The Passion of the Christ" was, for the most part, Biblically accurate. There are a few scenes in which "artistic license" was taken, but it was within the scope of the Biblical account. Examples of this "artistic license" were the demonic baby Satan was carrying, the demonic children tormenting Judas, and the woman wiping the blood off of Jesus' face on the way to the crucifixion site. Mary's role was overemphasized beyond what the Bible describes. As with any film based on the Bible, we should always compare what we see and hear with what the Bible actually says. Overall, if you see the movie "The Passion of the Christ" and read the Gospels (*Matthew, Mark, Luke,* and *John*) - you will find that the movie follows the Bible very closely.

$$\propto$$

8. Question: "Who was responsible for Christ's death?"

The answer to this question has many facets. First, there is no doubt the religious leaders of Israel were responsible for Jesus' death. *Matthew 26:3 & 4* tells us that *"the chief priests, and the scribes, and the elders of the people, assembled together to the palace of the high priest, who was called Caiaphas. And they consulted so that they might take Jesus by guile and kill Him."* The Jewish leaders demanded of the Romans that Jesus be put to death (*Matthew 27:22-25*). They couldn't continue to allow Him to work signs and wonders because it threatened their position and place in the religious society they dominated (*John 11:47-50*), so *"they plotted to put Him to death"* (*John 11:53*).

The Romans were the ones who actually crucified Him (*Matthew 27:27-37*). Crucifixion was a Roman method of execution, authorized and carried out by the Romans under the authority of Pontius Pilate, the Roman governor who sentenced Jesus. Roman soldiers drove the nails into His hands and feet, Roman troops erected the cross and a Roman solider pierced His side (*Matthew 27:27-35*).

The people of Israel were also complicit in the death of Jesus. They were the ones who shouted, *"Crucify Him! Crucify Him!"* as He stood on trial before Pilate (*Luke 23:21*). They also cried for the thief Barabbas to be released instead of Jesus (*Matthew 27:21*). Peter confirmed this in *Acts 2:22 & 23* when he told the men of Israel *"you have taken by lawless hands, have crucified and put to death"* Jesus of Nazareth. In fact the murder of Jesus was a conspiracy involving Rome, Herod, the Jewish leaders and the people of Israel, a diverse group of people who never worked together on anything before or since, but who came together this one time to plot and carry out the unthinkable – the murder of the son of God.

Ultimately, and perhaps somewhat amazingly, it was God Himself who put Jesus to death. This was the greatest act of divine justice ever carried out, done in *"the determined purpose and foreknowledge of God"* (*Acts 2:23*) and for the highest purpose. Jesus' death on the cross secured the salvation of countless millions and provided the only way God could forgive sin without compromising His holiness and perfect righteousness. Christ's death was God's perfect plan for the eternal redemption of His own. Far from being a victory for Satan, as some have suggested, or an unnecessary tragedy, it was the most gracious act of God's goodness and mercy, the ultimate expression of the Father's love for sinners. God put Jesus to death for our sin so that we could live in sinless righteousness before Him, righteousness only possible because of the cross. *"He made Him who knew no sin to be sin for us, that we might become the righteousness of God in Him"* (*2 Corinthians 5:21*).

So we who have come to Christ in faith are guilty of His blood, shed on the cross for us. He died to pay the penalty for our sins (*Romans 5:8; 6:23 & 24*). In the movie "The Passion of the Christ," the director,

Mel Gibson, was the one whose hands you see actually driving the nails through Christ's hands. He did it that way to remind himself, and everyone else, that it was our sins that nailed Jesus to the cross.

$$\infty$$

9. Question: "What trials did Jesus face before His crucifixion?"

The night of Jesus' arrest, He was brought before Annas, Caiaphas, and an assembly of religious leaders called the Sanhedrin (*John 18:19-24; Matthew 26:57*). After this He was taken before Pilate, the Roman Governor (*John 18:23*), sent off to Herod (*Luke 23:7*), and returned to Pilate (*Luke 23:11 & 12*), who finally sentenced Him to death.

There were six parts to Jesus' trial: three stages in a religious court and three stages before a Roman court. Jesus was tried before Annas, the former high priest; Caiaphas, the current high priest; and the Sanhedrin. He was charged in these "ecclesiastical" trials with blasphemy, claiming to be the Son of God, the Messiah.

The trials before Jewish authorities, the religious trials, showed the degree to which the Jewish leaders hated Him because they carelessly disregarded many of their own laws. There were several illegalities involved in these trials from the perspective of Jewish law:

$\Rightarrow$ No trial was to be held during feast time.
$\Rightarrow$ Each member of the court was to vote individually to convict or acquit, but Jesus was convicted by acclamation.
$\Rightarrow$ If the death penalty was given, a night must pass before the sentence was carried out; however, only a few hours passed before Jesus was placed on the Cross.
$\Rightarrow$ The Jews had no authority to execute anyone.
$\Rightarrow$ No trial was to be held at night, but this trial was held before dawn.
$\Rightarrow$ The accused was to be given counsel or representation, but Jesus had none.
$\Rightarrow$ The accused was not to be asked self-incriminating questions, but Jesus was asked if He was the Christ.

The trials before the Roman authorities started with Pilate (*John 18:23*) after Jesus was beaten. The charges brought against Him were very different from the charges in His religious trials. He was charged with inciting people to riot, forbidding the people to pay their taxes, and claiming to be King. Pilate found no reason to kill Jesus so he sent Him to Herod (*Luke 23:7*). Herod had Jesus ridiculed, but wanting to avoid the political liability, sent Jesus back to Pilate (*Luke 23:11 & 12*). This was the last trial as Pilate tried to appease the animosity of the Jews by having Jesus scourged. The Roman scourge is a terrible whipping of 39 lashes. In a final effort to have Jesus released, Pilate offered the prisoner Barabbas to be crucified and Jesus released, but to no avail. The crowds called for Barabbas to be released and Jesus to be crucified. Pilate granted their demand and surrendered Jesus to their will (*Luke 23:25*). The trials of Jesus represent the ultimate mockery of justice. Jesus, the most innocent man in the history of the world, was found guilty of crimes and sentenced to death by crucifixion.

$\propto$

10. Question: "Where was Jesus for the three days between His death and resurrection?"

1 Peter 3:18 & 19 states, *"For Christ also suffered once for sins, the just for the unjust, that He might bring us to God, being put to death in the flesh but made alive by the Spirit, by whom also He went and preached to the spirits in prison."* The phrase *"by the Spirit"* in *verse 18* is exactly the same construction as the phrase, *"in the flesh"* So it seems best to relate the word "spirit" to the same realm as the word "flesh." The flesh and spirit are Christ's flesh and spirit. The words *"made alive by (in) the spirit,"* point to the fact that Christ's sin-bearing and death brought about the separation of His human spirit from the Father (*Matthew 27:46*). The contrast is between flesh and spirit, as in *Matthew 27:46* and Romans *1:3-4*, and not between Christ's flesh and the Holy Spirit. When Christ's atonement for sin was completed, His spirit resumed the fellowship which had been broken.

First *Peter 3:18-22* describes a necessary link between Christ's suffering (*verse 18*) and His glorification (*verse 22*). Only Peter gives specific information about what happened between these two events. The word *"preached"* in *verse 19* is not the usual word in the New Testament to describe the preaching of the gospel. It literally means to herald a message. Jesus suffered and died on the Cross, His body being put to death, and His spirit died when He was made sin. But His spirit was made alive and He yielded it to the Father. According to Peter, sometime between His death and His resurrection Jesus made a special proclamation to *"the spirits in prison."*

To begin with, Peter referred to people as *"souls"* and not *"spirits"* *(3:20)*. In the New Testament, the word "spirits" is used to describe angels or demons, not human beings; and *verse 22* seems to bear out this meaning. Also, nowhere in the Bible are we told that Jesus visited hell. *Acts 2:31* says that He went to *"Hades"* (*New American Standard Bible*), but "Hades" is not hell. The word "Hades" refers to the realm of the dead, a temporary place where they await the resurrection. *Revelation 20:11-15* in the NASB or the New International Version give a clear distinction between the two. Hell is the permanent and final place of judgment for the lost. Hades is a temporary place.

Our Lord yielded His spirit to the Father, died, and at some time between death and resurrection, visited the realm of the dead where He delivered a message to spirit beings, *probably fallen angels; see Jude 6*, who were somehow related to the period before the flood in Noah's time. *Verse 20* makes this clear. Peter did not tell us what He proclaimed to these imprisoned spirits, but it could not be a message of redemption since angels cannot be saved (*Hebrews 2:16*). It was probably a declaration of victory over Satan and his hosts (*1 Peter 3:22; Colossians 2:15*). *Ephesians 4:8-10* also seems to indicate that Christ went to "paradise" (*Luke 16:20; 23:43*) and took to heaven all those who had believed in Him prior to His death. The passage doesn't give a great amount of detail about what occurred, but most Bible scholars agree that this is what is meant by "led captivity captive."

So, all that is to say, the Bible isn't entirely clear what exactly Christ did for the three days between His death and resurrection. It does seem, though, that He was preaching victory over the fallen angels and/or unbelievers. What we can know for sure is that Jesus was not giving people a second chance for salvation. The Bible tells us that we face judgment after death (*Hebrews 9:27*), not a second chance. There isn't really any definitively clear answer for what Jesus was doing for the time between His death and resurrection. Perhaps this is one of the mysteries we will understand once we reach glory.

11. Question: "Why did Jesus have to experience so much suffering?"

Isaiah 52:14 declares, *"Just as there were many who were appalled at Him — His appearance was so disfigured beyond that of any man and his form marred beyond human likeness."* Jesus suffered most severely throughout the trials, torture, and crucifixion (*Matthew chapter 27, Mark chapter 15, Luke chapter 23, John chapter 19*). As horrible as His physical suffering was, it was nothing compared to the spiritual suffering He went through. *2 Corinthians 5:21, "God made him who had no sin to be sin for us, so that in him we might become the righteousness of God."* Jesus had the weight of the sins of the entire world on Him (*1 John 2:2*). It was sin that caused Jesus to cry out, *"My God, my God, why have you forsaken me?" (Matthew 27:46)*. So, as brutal as Jesus' physical suffering was, it was nothing compared to His having to bear our sins - and die for our sins (*Romans 5:8*).

Isaiah chapter 53, verses 3 and 5 especially predict Jesus' suffering, *"He was despised and rejected by men, a man of sorrows, and familiar with suffering. Like one from whom men hide their faces he was despised, and we esteemed him not. But he was pierced for our transgressions, he was crushed for our iniquities; the punishment that brought us peace was upon him, and by his wounds we are healed." Psalm 22:14-18* is another powerful passage predicting the suffering of the Messiah, *"I am poured out like water, and all my bones are out of joint. My heart has turned to wax; it has melted away within me. My strength is dried up like a potsherd, and my tongue sticks to the roof of my mouth; you lay me in the dust of death. Dogs have surrounded me; a band of evil men has encircled me, they have pierced my hands and my feet. I can count all my bones; people stare and gloat over me. They divide my garments among them and cast lots for my clothing."*

Why did Jesus have to suffer so badly? Some think that Jesus' physical torture was part of His being punished for our sins, in our place. To some extent, this is likely the case. At the same time, the torture Jesus underwent speaks more of the hatred and cruelty of humanity than it does of God's punishment for sin. Satan's absolute hatred of God and Jesus was surely a part of the motivation behind the relentless torture and abuse. Jesus' suffering is the ultimate example of how sinful men feel towards a holy God (*Romans 3:10-18*).

12. Question: "Did Jesus have brothers and sisters (siblings)?"

Jesus' brothers are mentioned in several Bible verses. *Matthew 12:46, Luke 8:19*, and *Mark 3:31* say that Jesus' mother and brothers came to see Him. The Bible tells us that Jesus had four brothers: James, Joseph, Simon, and Judas (*Matthew 13:55*). The Bible also tells us that Jesus had sisters, but they are not named or numbered (*Matthew 13:56*). In *John 7:1-10*, His brothers go on to the festival while Jesus stays behind. In *Acts 1:14*, His brothers and mother are described as praying with the disciples. Later, in *Galatians 1:19*, it mentions that James was Jesus' brother. The most natural conclusion of these passages is to interpret that Jesus had actual blood siblings.

Some Roman Catholics claim that these "brothers" were actually Jesus' cousins. However, in each instance, the specific Greek word for "brother" is used. While the word can refer to other relatives, its normal and literal meaning is a physical brother. There was a Greek word for cousin, and it was not used. Further, if they were Jesus' cousins, why would they so often be described as being with Mary, Jesus' mother? There is nothing in the context of His mother and brothers coming to see Him that even hints that they were anyone other than His literal, blood-related half-brothers.

A second Roman Catholic argument is that Jesus' brothers and sisters were the children of Joseph from a previous marriage, before he married Mary. An entire theory of Joseph's being significantly older than Mary, having been previously married, having multiple children, and then being widowed before marrying Mary is invented. The problem with this is that the Bible does not even hint that Joseph was married or had children before he married Mary. If Joseph had at least six children before he married Mary, why are they not mentioned in Joseph and Mary's trip to Bethlehem (*Luke 2:4-7*) or their trip to Egypt (*Matthew 2:13-15*) or their trip back to Nazareth (*Matthew 2:20-23*)?

There is no Biblical reason to believe that these siblings are anything other than the actual children of Joseph and Mary. Those who oppose the idea that Jesus had half-brothers and half-sisters do so, not from a reading of Scripture, but from a preconceived concept of the perpetual virginity of Mary, which is itself clearly unbiblical: "But he (Joseph) had no union with her (Mary) UNTIL she gave birth to a son. And he gave Him the name Jesus" (*Matthew 1:25*). Jesus had half-siblings, half-brothers and half-sisters, who were the children of Joseph and

Mary. That is the clear and unambiguous teaching of God's Word.

$$\infty$$

13. Question: "Did Jesus go to hell between His death and resurrection?"

Did Jesus' soul go to Hell during the time in between His death and resurrection? There is a great deal of confusion in regards to this question. This concept comes primarily from the Apostles' Creed, which states, "He descended into Hell." There are also a few Scriptures which, depending on how they are translated, describe Jesus going to "Hell." In studying this issue, it is important to first understand what the Bible teaches about the "realms" of the dead.

In the Hebrew Scriptures, the word used to describe the realm of the dead is "Sheol." It simply means the "place of the dead" or the "place of departed souls/spirits." The New Testament Greek word that is used for hell is "Hades," which also refers to "the place of the dead." Other Scriptures in the New Testament indicate that Sheol/Hades is a temporary place, where souls are kept as they await the final resurrection and judgment. *Revelation 20:11-15* gives a clear distinction between the two. Hell (the lake of fire) is the permanent and final place of judgment for the lost. Hades is a temporary place. So, no, Jesus did not go to "Hell" because "Hell" is a future realm, only put into effect after the Great White Throne Judgment (*Revelation 20:11-15*).

Sheol/Hades is a realm with two divisions (*Matthew 11:23; 16:18; Luke 10:15; 16:23; Acts 2:27-31*), the abodes of the saved and the lost. The abode of the saved was called "Paradise" and "Abraham's bosom." The abodes of the saved and the lost are separated by a "great gulf fixed" (*Luke 16:26*). When Jesus ascended to Heaven, He took the occupants of Paradise (believers) with Him (*Ephesians 4:8-10*). The lost side of Sheol/Hades has remained unchanged. All unbelieving dead go there awaiting their final judgment in the future. Did Jesus go to Sheol/Hades? Yes, according to Ephesians *4:8-10* and *1 Peter 3:18-20*.

Some of the confusion has arisen from such passages as *Psalm 16:10-11*, "For thou wilt not leave my soul in hell; neither wilt thou suffer thine Holy One to see corruption....Thou wilt show me the path of life..." "Hell" is not a correct translation of this verse. A correct reading would be "the grave" or "Sheol." Jesus said years later on the Cross to the thief beside Him, "Today, thou shalt be with Me in Paradise." His body was in the tomb; His soul/spirit went to the "Paradise" realm of Sheol/Hades. He then removed all the righteous dead from Paradise and took them with Him to Heaven. Unfortunately, in many translations of the Bible, translators are not consistent, or correct, in how they translate the Hebrew and Greek words for "Sheol," "Hades," and "Hell."

Some have the viewpoint that Jesus went to "Hell" or the suffering side of Sheol/Hades in order to further be punished for our sins. This idea is completely unbiblical! It was the death of Jesus on the Cross and His suffering in our place that sufficiently provided for our redemption. It was His shed blood that substantiated our own cleansing from sin (*1 John 1:7-9*). As He hung there on the Cross, He took the sin burden of the whole human race upon Himself. *"He became sin for us,"* 2 Corinthians 5:21 states: *"For He hath made Him to be sin for us Who knew no sin; that we might be made the righteousness of God in Him."* This imputation of sin helps us understand Christ's struggle in the garden of Gethsemane with the cup of sin which would be poured out upon Him on the cross.

When Jesus cried upon the Cross, "Oh, Father, why have You forsaken Me?" it was then He was separated from the Father because of the sin poured out upon Him. As He gave up His spirit, He said, "Father, into Your hands I commit My spirit." His suffering was completed in our stead. His soul/spirit went to the Paradise side of Hades. Jesus did not go to Hell. Jesus' suffering ended the moment He died. The payment for sin was paid. He then awaited the resurrection of His body and His return to His glory in His ascension. Did Jesus go to Hell? No. Did Jesus go to Sheol/Hades? Yes.

α

14. Question: "Is Jesus God? Did Jesus ever claim to be God?"

Jesus is never recorded in the Bible as saying the exact words, "I am

God." That does not mean, however, that He did not proclaim that He is God. Take for example Jesus' words in *John 10:30, "I and the Father are one."* At first glance, this might not seem to be a claim to be God. However, look at the Jews' reaction to His statement, *"We are not stoning you for any of these, replied the Jews, but for blasphemy, because you, a mere man, claim to be God" (John 10:33)*. The Jews understood Jesus' statement to be a claim to be God. In the following verses, Jesus never corrects the Jews by saying, "I did not claim to be God." That indicates Jesus was truly saying He was God by declaring, *"I and the Father are one" (John 10:30)*. John 8:58 is another example. Jesus declared, *"I tell you the truth, before Abraham was born, I am!"* Again, in response, the Jews take up stones in an attempt to stone Jesus *(John 8:59)*. Why would the Jews want to stone Jesus if He hadn't said something they believed to be blasphemous, namely, a claim to be God?

John 1:1 says that *"the Word was God." John 1:14* says that *"the Word became flesh."* This clearly indicates that Jesus is God in the flesh. *Acts 20:28* tells us, *"...Be shepherds of the church of God, which He bought with His own blood."* Who bought the church with His own blood? Jesus Christ. *Acts 20:28* declares that God purchased the church with His own blood. Therefore, Jesus is God!

Thomas the disciple declared concerning Jesus, *"Lord and my God" (John 20:28)*. Jesus does not correct him. *Titus 2:13* encourages us to wait for the coming of our God and Savior - Jesus Christ (see also *2 Peter 1:1*). In *Hebrews 1:8*, the Father declares of Jesus, *"But about the Son He says, "Your throne, O God, will last forever and ever, and righteousness will be the scepter of your kingdom.""*

In Revelation, an angel instructed the Apostle John to only worship God *(Revelation 19:10)*. Several times in Scripture Jesus receives worship *(Matthew 2:11; 14:33; 28:9, 17; Luke 24:52; John 9:38)*. He never rebukes people for worshiping Him. If Jesus were not God, He would have told people to not worship Him, just as the angel in Revelation had. There are many other verses and passages of Scripture that argue for Jesus' deity.

The most important reason that Jesus has to be God is that if He is not God, His death would not have been sufficient to pay the penalty for the sins of the whole world *(1 John 2:2)*. Only God could pay such an infinite penalty. Only God could take on the sins of the world *(2 Corin-*

thians 5:21), die, and be resurrected - proving His victory over sin and death.

⟨◯

15. Question: "Is the deity of Christ Biblical?"

In addition to Jesus' specific claims about Himself (see Is Jesus God?), His disciples also acknowledged the deity of Christ. They claimed that Jesus had the right to forgive sins - something only God can do, as it is God who is offended by sin (*Acts 5:31; Colossians 3:13; cf. Psalm 130:4; Jeremiah 31:34).* In close connection with this last claim, Jesus is also said to be the one who will "judge the living and the dead" (*2 Timothy 4:1*). Thomas cried out to Jesus, "my Lord and my God!" (*John 20:28*). Paul calls Jesus "great God and Savior" (*Titus 2:13*), and points out that prior to His incarnation Jesus existed in the "form of God" (*Philippians 2:5–8*). The writer to the Hebrews says regarding Jesus that *"Your throne, O God, will last forever and ever"* (*Hebrews 1:8*). John states that, *"In the beginning was the Word, and the Word was with God, and the Word [Jesus] was God"* (*John 1:1*). Examples of Scriptures that teach the deity of Christ could be multiplied (*see Revelation 1:17; 2:8; 22:13; 1 Corinthians 10:4; 1 Peter 2:6–8; cf. Psalm 18:2; 95:1; 1 Peter 5:4; Hebrews 13:20*), but even one of these is enough to show that Christ was considered to be deity by His followers.

Jesus is also given titles that are unique to Yahweh (the formal name of God) in the Old Testament. The Old Testament title "redeemer" (*Psalm 130:7; Hosea 13:14*) is used of Jesus in the New Testament (*Titus 2:13; Revelation 5:9*). Jesus is called Immanuel (*"God with us" in Matthew 1*). In *Zechariah 12:10*, it is Yahweh who says, *"They will look on me, the one they have pierced."* But the New Testament applies this to Jesus' crucifixion (*John 19:37; Revelation 1:7*). If it is Yahweh who is pierced and looked upon, and Jesus was the one pierced and looked upon, then Jesus is Yahweh. Paul interprets *Isaiah 45:22 & 23* as applying to Jesus in *Philippians 2:10 & 11*. Further, Jesus' name is used alongside Yahweh's in prayer *"Grace and peace to you from God our Father and the Lord Jesus Christ"* (*Galatians 1:3; Ephesians 1:2*). This would be blasphemy if

Christ were not deity. The name of Jesus appears with Yahweh's in Jesus' commanded to baptize "in the name [singular] of the Father and of the Son and of the Holy Spirit" (*Matthew 28:19; see also 2 Corinthians 13:14.*

Actions that can be accomplished only by God are credited to Jesus. Jesus not only raised the dead (*John 5:21; 11:38–44*), and forgave sins (*Acts 5:31; 13:38*), He created and sustains the universe (*John 1:2; Colossians 1:16-17*)! This point is made even more forceful when one considers that Yahweh said He was alone during creation (*Isaiah 44:24*). Further, Christ possesses attributes that only deity can have: eternality (*John 8:58*), omnipresence (*Matthew 18:20, 28:20*), omniscience (*Matthew 16:21*), omnipotence (*John 11:38-44*).

Now, it is one thing to claim to be God or to fool someone into believing it is true, and something else entirely to prove it to be so. Christ offered as proof of His claim to deity many miracles and even rose from the dead. Just a few of Jesus' miracles include turning water to wine (*John 2:7*), walking on water (*Matthew 14:25*), multiplying physical objects (*John 6:11*), healing the blind (*John 9:7*), the lame (*Mark 2:3*), and the sick (*Matthew 9:35; Mark 1:40–42*), and even raising people from the dead (*John 11:43–44; Luke 7:11–15; Mark 5:35*). Moreover, Christ Himself rose from the dead. Far from the so-called dying and rising gods of pagan mythology, nothing like the resurrection is seriously claimed by other religions - and no other claim has as much extra-scriptural confirmation. According to Dr. Gary Habermas, there are at least twelve historical facts that even non-Christian critical scholars will admit:

⇒ Jesus died by crucifixion.
⇒ He was buried
⇒ His death caused the disciples to despair and lose hope.
⇒ Jesus' tomb was discovered (or claimed to be discovered) to be empty a few days later.
⇒ The disciples believed they experienced appearances of the risen Jesus.
⇒ After this the disciples were transformed from doubters into bold believers.
⇒ This message was the center of preaching in the early Church.
⇒ This message was preached in Jerusalem.
⇒ As a result of this preaching, the Church was born and it grew.

- ⇒ Resurrection day, Sunday, replaced the Sabbath (Saturday) as the primary day of worship.
- ⇒ James, a skeptic, was converted when he also believed that he saw the resurrected Jesus.
- ⇒ Paul, an enemy of Christianity, was converted by an experience which he believed to be an appearance of the risen Jesus.

Even if someone were to object to this specific list, only a few are needed to prove the resurrection and establish the gospel: Jesus' death, burial, resurrection, and appearances (*1 Corinthians 15:1-5*). While there may be some theories to explain one or two of the above facts, only the resurrection explains and accounts for them all. Critics admit that the disciples claimed they saw the risen Jesus. Neither lies nor hallucinations can transform people the way the resurrection did. First, what would they have had to gain? Christianity wasn't popular and it certainly did not make them any money. Second, liars do not make good martyrs. There is no better explanation than the resurrection for the disciples' willingness to die horrible deaths for their faith. Yes, lots of people die for lies that they think are true, but no one dies for what they know is untrue.

In conclusion: Christ claimed He was Yahweh, He was deity (not just "a god" - but the True God), His followers (Jews who would have been terrified of idolatry) believed Him and referred to Him as such. Christ proved His claims to deity through miracles including the world-altering resurrection. No other hypothesis can explain these facts.

16. Question: "What is the hypostatic union? How can Jesus be both God and man at the same time?"

Answer: The hypostatic union is the term used to describe how God the Son, Jesus Christ, took on a human nature, yet remained fully God at the same time. Jesus always had been God (John 8:58; 10:30), but at the incarnation Jesus took on human flesh - He became a human being (John 1:14). The addition of the human nature to the divine nature is Jesus, the God-man. This is the hypostatic union, Jesus Christ, one

Person, fully God and fully man.

Jesus' two natures, human and divine, are inseparable. Jesus will for-ever be the God-man, fully God and fully human, two distinct natures in one Person. Jesus' humanity and divinity are not mixed, but are united without loss of separate identity. Jesus sometimes operated with the limitations of humanity (John 4:6; 19:28) and other times in the power of His deity (John 11:43; Matthew 14:18-21). In both, Jesus' actions were from His one Person. Jesus had two natures, but only one person or personality.

The doctrine of the hypostatic union is an attempt to explain how Jesus could be both God and man at the same time. It is ultimately, though, a doctrine that we are incapable of fully understanding. It is impossible for us to fully understand how God works. We, as finite human beings, should not expect to be able to comprehend an infinite God. Jesus is God's Son in that He was conceived by the Holy Spirit (Luke 1:35). But that does not mean Jesus did not exist before He was conceived. Jesus always has existed (John 8:58; 10:30). When Jesus was con-ceived, He became a human being in addition to being God (John 1:1,14).

Jesus is both God and man. Jesus has always been God, but He did not become a human being until He was conceived in Mary. Jesus became a human being so that He could identify with us in our struggles (Hebrews 2:17) and, more importantly, so that He could die on the cross to pay the penalty for our sins (Philippians 2:5-11). In summary, the hypostatic union teaches that Jesus is both fully human and fully divine, that there is no mixture or dilution of either nature, and that He is one united Person, forever.

17. Question: "On what day was Jesus crucified?"

The Bible does not specifically state which day of the week Jesus was crucified. The two most widely held views are Friday and Wednesday. Some, however, using a synthesis of both the Friday and Wednesday arguments, accept Thursday as the day.

Jesus said in *Matthew 12:40, "For as Jonah was three days and three nights in the belly of the great fish, so will the Son of Man be three days and three nights in the heart of the earth."* Those who argue for a Friday crucifixion say that there is still a valid way in which He could have been considered in the grave for three days. In the Jewish mind of the First Century, a part of day was considered as a full day. Since Jesus was in the grave for part of Friday, all of Saturday, and part of Sunday, He could be considered to have been in the grave for three days. One of the principal arguments for Friday is found in *Mark 15:42* that notes Jesus was crucified *"the day before the Sabbath."* If that was the weekly Sabbath, i.e. Saturday, then that fact leads to a Friday crucifixion. Another argument for Friday says that verses such as *Matthew 16:21* and *Luke 9:22* teach that Jesus would rise on the third day; therefore, He wouldn't need to be in the grave a full three days and nights. But while some translations use "on the third day" for these verses, not all do and not everyone agrees that that is the best way to translate these verses. Furthermore, *Mark 8:31* states that Jesus will be raised *"after"* three days.

The Thursday argument expands on the Friday view and argues mainly that there are too many events (some count as many as twenty) happening between Christ's burial and Sunday morning to occur from Friday evening to Sunday morning. They point out that this is especially a problem when the only full day between Friday and Sunday was Saturday, the Jewish Sabbath. An extra day or two eliminates that problem. The Thursday advocates could reason: Suppose you haven't seen a friend since Monday evening. The next time you see him it is Thursday morning and you say, "I haven't seen you in three days" even though it had technically only been 60 hours (2.5 days). If Jesus was crucified on Thursday, this example shows how it could be considered three days.

The Wednesday opinion states that there were two Sabbaths that week. After the first one (the one that occurred on the evening of the crucifixion, *Mark 15:42; Luke 23:52-54*), the women purchased spices--note that they made their purchase after the Sabbath (*Mark 16:1*). The Wednesday view holds that this "Sabbath" was the Passover (see *Lev 16:29-31; 23:24-32, 39* where high holy days that are not necessarily the seventh day of the week are referred to as the Sabbath). The second Sabbath that week was the normal weekly Saturday. Note that in *Luke 23:56*, the women who had purchased spices after the first Sabbath, returned and prepared the spices then "rested on the Sabbath" (*Luke 23:56*). The argument states that they could not purchase the spices after the Sabbath, yet prepare those spices before the Sabbath—unless there were two Sabbaths. With the two-Sabbath view, if Christ was crucified on Thursday, then the high holy Sabbath (the Passover) would have begun Thursday at sundown and ended at Friday sundown—at the beginning of the weekly Sabbath or Saturday. Purchasing the spices after the first Sabbath (Passover) would have meant they purchased them on Saturday and were breaking the Sabbath.

Therefore, this view states, the only explanation that does not violate the biblical account of the women and the spices and holds to a literal understanding of *Matthew 12:40*, is that Christ was crucified on Wednesday. The Sabbath that was a high holy day (Passover) occurred on Thursday, the women purchased spices (after that) on Friday and returned and prepared the spices on the same day, they rested on Saturday which was the weekly Sabbath, then brought the spices to the tomb early Sunday. He was buried near sundown on Wednesday, which began Thursday in the Jewish calendar. Using a Jewish calendar, you have Thursday night (night one), Thursday day (day one), Friday night (night two), Friday day (day two), Saturday night (night three), Saturday day (day three). We don't know exactly when He rose, but we do know that it was before sunrise on Sunday (*John 20:1*, Mary Magdalene came *"while it was still dark"* and the stone was rolled away and she found Peter and told him that *"they have taken away the Lord out of the tomb"*), so He could have risen as early as just after sunset Saturday evening, which began the first day of the week to the Jews.

A possible problem with the Wednesday view is that the disciples who walked with Jesus on the road to Emmaus did so on "the same day" of His resurrection (*Luke 24:13*). The disciples, who do not recognize Jesus, tell Him of Jesus' crucifixion (*24:21*) and say that "today is the third day since these things happened" (*24:22*). Wednesday to Sunday is four days. A possible explanation is that they may have been counting since Wednesday evening at Christ's burial, which begins the Jewish Thursday, and Thursday to Sunday could be counted as three days.

In the grand scheme of things, it is not all that important to know what day of the week Christ was crucified. If it were very important, then God's Word would have clearly communicated the day. What is important is that He did die, and that He physically, bodily rose from the dead. What is equally important is the reason He died to take the punishment that all sinners deserve. *John 3:16* and *3:36* both proclaim that believing, or putting your trust, in Him results in eternal life!

18. Question: "Why is the Virgin Birth so important?"

The doctrine of the virgin birth is crucially important (*Isaiah 7:14; Matthew 1:23; Luke 1:27 & 34*). First, let's look at how scripture describes the blessed event. In response to Mary's query, "how?" Gabriel says, *"The Holy Ghost shall come upon thee, and the power of the Highest shall overshadow thee" (Luke 1:35)*. The angel encourages Joseph to marry Mary with these words: *"that which is conceived in her is of the Holy Ghost" (Matthew 1:20)*. Matthew states that the virgin *"was found with child of the Holy Ghost" (Matthew 1:18)*. *Galatians 4:4* also teaches the Virgin Birth: *"God sent forth His Son, made of a woman."*

From these passages, it is certainly clear that Jesus' birth was the result of the Holy Spirit working within Mary's body. The immaterial (the Spirit) and the material (Mary's womb) were both involved. Mary, of course, could not impregnate herself, and in that sense she was simply a "vessel." Only God could perform the miracle of the Incarnation.

Denying a physical connection between Mary and Jesus would imply that Jesus was not truly human. Scripture teaches that Jesus was fully human, with a physical body like ours. This He received from Mary. At the same time, Jesus was fully God, with an eternal, sinless nature. See *John 1:14; 1 Timothy 3:16*; and *Hebrews 2:14-17*.

Jesus was not born in sin; that is, He had no sin nature (*Hebrews 7:26*). It would seem that the sin nature is passed down from generation to generation through the father (*Romans 5:12, 17, 19*). The Virgin Birth circumvented the transmission of the sin nature and allowed the eternal God to become a perfect man.

19. Question: "What did Jesus look like?"

The Bible never gives any physical description of Christ. The closest thing we get to a description is in *Isaiah 53:2b, "He had no beauty or majesty to attract us to Him, nothing in His appearance that we should desire Him."* All this tells us is that Jesus' appearance was just like any other man's. He was ordinary looking. Isaiah was here prophesying that the coming suffering Servant would arise in lowly conditions and wear none of the usual emblems of royalty, making His true identity visible only to the discerning eye of faith.

Isaiah further describes the appearance of Christ as He would appear as He was being scourged prior to His crucifixion. *"His appearance was so disfigured beyond that of any man and his form marred beyond human likeness" (Isaiah 52:14).* These words describe the inhuman cruelty He suffered to the point that He no longer looked like a human being (*Matthew 26:67; 27:30; John 19:3*). His appearance was so awful that people looked at Him in astonishment.

Most of the images we have of Jesus today are probably not accurate. Jesus was a Jew, so He likely had dark skin, dark eyes, and dark hair. This is a far cry from the blond-haired, blue-eyed, fair-skinned Jesus in many modern pictures. One thing is clear: if it were important for us to know what He really did look like, Matthew, Peter and John, who spent three years with Him, would certainly be able to give us an accurate description, as would His own brothers, James and Jude. Yet, these New Testament writers offer no details about His physical attributes.

20. Question: "When did Jesus know that He was God?"

The Bible does not clearly state that there was a point at which He knew that He was the second Person of the Trinity. At some point, Jesus fully realized who He was from eternity past, expressing it this way: *"Jesus said to them, "Most assuredly, I say to you, before Abraham was, I AM." (John 8:58). "And now, O Father, glorify Me together with Yourself, with the glory which I had with You before the world was." (John 17:5).* But the pre-incarnate Christ always knew He was the second Person of the Trinity. He made the worlds: *"(God) has in these last days spoken to us by His Son, whom He has appointed heir of all things, through whom also He made the worlds" (Hebrews 1:2).* Jesus knew from the foundation of the world that He would die for our sins: *"Between you and the woman, And between your seed and her Seed; He shall bruise your head, and you shall bruise His* heel." *(Genesis 3:15)*, and *"..... the Lamb slain from the foundation of the world" (Revelation 13:8)*.

While we do not have a clear scripture revealing the thoughts of Jesus as a baby, we can at least discover from Scripture that as a young child He was well aware of His work. Jesus was preparing even as a boy to finish the work His Father sent Him to do. When His parents were concerned about His being missing on a trip to Jerusalem, they found Him in the temple *"sitting in the midst of the teachers, both listening to them and asking them questions." (Luke 2:46)*. When asked why He would disappear and worry them so, He told His parents: *"'Why did you seek Me? Did you not know that I must be about My Father's business?' But they did not understand the statement which He spoke to them." (Luke 2:49-50)*. Joseph and Mary may not have understood, but Jesus certainly did understand at the age of twelve that He was the Son of God and that the Father had foreordained the work He was to do.

After the incident in the temple, we are told *"And Jesus increased in wisdom and stature, and in favor with God and men" (Luke 2:52)*. If at this point in Jesus' experience He knew everything, it would not follow logically that He would need to "increase in wisdom." We know He had to grow physically (in stature), but we must also believe the scripture where our understanding fails us, that is, that He also put Himself voluntarily in a position where He needed to assimilate knowledge as a man. He needed to be truly man. He was always God, but He needed to become in all ways, except for sin, a man as well. In theological terms we refer to this as the hypostatic union. In order for Him to have a legitimate experience of temptation, He needed to limit certain facets of divine advantage. In this He emptied Himself of all His observable physical characteristics of divinity such as described in Revelation: *"His head and his hairs were white like wool, as white as snow; and his eyes were as a flame of fire; And his feet like unto fine brass, as if they burned in a furnace; and his voice as the sound of many waters" (Revelation 1:14-15)*. We know this to be true because Isaiah describes Him in this way: *"For He shall grow up before Him as a tender plant, And as a root out of dry ground. He has no form or comeliness; And when we see Him, There is no beauty that we should desire Him. " (Isaiah 53:2)*.

We can conclude that although the pre-incarnate Jesus knew from eternity past who He was and what His work in the world was to be, the incarnate Jesus came to that realization at some point in His earthly life. Just what that point was, we cannot know for sure.

21. Question: "Where does the Old Testament mention Christ?"

Answer: There are many Old Testament prophecies about Jesus Christ. Some interpreters place the number of Messianic prophecies in the hundreds. Following are those that are considered the clearest and most important. Regarding Jesus' birth: *Isaiah 7:14, "Therefore the Lord himself will give you a sign: The virgin will be with child and will give birth to a son, and will call him Immanuel." Isaiah 9:6, "For to us a child is born, to us a son is given, and the government will be on his shoulders. And he will be called Wonderful Counselor, Mighty God, Everlasting Father, Prince of Peace." Micah 5:2, "But you, Bethlehem Ephrathah, though you are small among the clans of Judah, out of you will come for me one who will be ruler over Israel, whose origins are from of old, from ancient times."*

Concerning Jesus' ministry and death: *Zechariah 9:9, "Rejoice greatly, O Daughter of Zion! Shout, Daughter of Jerusalem! See, your king comes to you, righteous and having salvation, gentle and riding on a donkey, on a colt, the foal of a donkey." Psalm 22:16-18, "Dogs have surrounded me; a band of evil men has encircled me, they have pierced my hands and my feet. I can count all my bones; people stare and gloat over me. They divide my garments among them and cast lots for my clothing."*

Likely the clearest prophecy about Jesus, and definitely the longest, is the entire *53rd chapter of Isaiah. Isaiah 53:3-7, "He was despised and rejected by men, a man of sorrows, and familiar with suffering. Like one from whom men hide their faces he was despised, and we esteemed him not. Surely he took up our infirmities and carried our sorrows, yet we considered him stricken by God, smitten by him, and afflicted. But he was pierced for our transgressions, he was crushed for our iniquities; the punishment that brought us peace was upon him, and by his wounds we are healed. We all, like sheep, have gone astray, each of us has turned to his own way; and the LORD has laid on him the iniquity of us all. He was oppressed and afflicted, yet he did not open his mouth; he was led like a lamb to the slaughter, and as a sheep before her shearers is silent, so he did not open his mouth."*

The "seventy sevens" prophecy in *Daniel chapter 9* predicted the precise date that Jesus, the Messiah, would be "cut off." *Isaiah 50:6* accurately describes the beating that Jesus endured. *Zechariah 12:10* predicts the "piercing" of the Messiah, which occurred after Jesus died on the cross. Many more examples could be provided, but these will suffice. The Old Testament most definitely prophesies the coming of Jesus as the Messiah.

22. Question: "What happened during Jesus' childhood?"

Other than *Luke 2:41-52*, the Bible does not tell us anything about Jesus' youth. From this incident we do know certain things about Jesus' childhood. First, He was the son of parents who were devout in their religious observances. As required by their faith, Joseph and Mary made the yearly pilgrimage to Jerusalem for the Feast of the Passover. In addition, they brought their 12-year-old son to celebrate His first Feast in preparation for His bar mitzvah at age 13, when Jewish boys commemorate their passage into adulthood. Here we see a typical boy in a typical family of that day.

We see also in this story that Jesus' lingering in the temple was neither mischievous nor disobedient, but a natural result of His knowledge that He must be about His Father's business. That He was astonishing the temple teachers with His wisdom and knowledge speaks to His extraordinary abilities, while His listening and asking questions of His elders shows that He was utterly respectful, taking the role of a student as was fitting for a child of His age.

From this incident to His baptism at age 30, all we know of Jesus' youth was that He left Jerusalem and returned to Nazareth with His parents and *"was obedient to them" Luke 2:51*. He fulfilled His duty to His earthly parents in submission to the 5th commandment, an essential part of the perfect obedience to the Law of Moses which He rendered on our behalf. Beyond that, all we know is that *"Jesus grew in wisdom and stature, and in favor with God and men" (Luke 2:52).*

Evidently, this is all God determined that we needed to know. There are some extra-Biblical writings which contain stories of Jesus' youth (the Gospel of Thomas, for example). But we have no way of knowing whether any of these stories are true and reliable. God chose not to tell us much about Jesus' childhood, so we have to just trust Him that nothing occurred which we need to know about.

23. Question: "Could Jesus have sinned? If He was not capable of sinning, how could He truly be able to 'sympathize with our weaknesses' *(Hebrews 4:15)*? **If He could not sin, what was the point of the temptation?"**

This question is divided into two categories. It is important to remember that this is not a question of whether Jesus sinned. Both sides agree, as the Bible clearly says, that Jesus did not sin. The question is whether Jesus could have sinned. Those who hold to impeccability believe that Jesus could not have sinned. Those who hold to peccability believe that Jesus could have sinned, but did not. Which view is correct? The clear teaching of Scripture is that Jesus was impeccable, Jesus could not have sinned. If He could have sinned, He would still be able to sin today because He retains the same essence He did while living on earth. He is the God-Man and will forever remain so, having full deity and full humanity so included in one person as to be indivisible. To believe that Jesus could sin is to believe that God could sin. *Colossians 1:19, "For it pleased the Father that in Him all the fullness should dwell." Colossians 2:9, "For in Him dwells all the fullness of the Godhead bodily."*

Although Jesus is fully human, He was not born with the same sinful nature that we are born with. He certainly was tempted in the same way we are, in that temptations were put before Him by Satan, yet remained sinless because God is incapable of sinning. It is against His very nature *(Matthew 4:1; Hebrews 2:18, 4:15; James 1:13)*. Sin is by definition a trespass of the Law. God created the Law, and the Law is by nature what God would or would not do; therefore, sin is anything that God would not do by His very nature.

To be tempted is not in and of itself sinful. A person could tempt you with something you have no desire to do, such as committing murder or participating in sexual perversions. You probably have no desire whatsoever to take part in these actions, but you were still tempted because someone placed the possibility before you. There are at least two definitions for tempted:

⇒ Tempted - To have a sinful proposition suggested to you by someone or something outside yourself or by your own sin nature.

⇒ Tempted - To consider actually participating in a sinful act and the possible pleasures and consequences of such an act to the degree that the act is already taking place in your mind.

The first definition does not describe a sinful act/thought, the second does. When you dwell upon a sinful act and consider how you might be able to bring it to pass, you have crossed the line of sin. Jesus was tempted in the fashion of definition 1, except that He was never tempted by a sin nature because it did not exist within Him. Satan proposed certain sinful acts to Jesus, but He had no inner desire to participate in the sin. Hence, He was tempted like we are but remained sinless.

Those who hold to peccability believe that if Jesus could not have sinned, He could not have truly experienced temptation, and therefore could not truly empathize with our struggles and temptations against sin. We have to remember that one does not have to experience something in order to understand it. God knows everything about everything. While God has never had the desire to sin, and has most definitely never sinned, God knows and understands what sin is. God knows and understands what it is like to be tempted. Jesus can empathize with our temptations because He knows...not because He has "experienced" all the same things we have.

Jesus knows what it is like to be tempted, but He does not know what it is like to sin. This does not prevent Him from assisting us. We are tempted with sins that are common to man (*1 Corinthians 10:13*). These sins generally can be boiled down to three different types: the lust of the eyes, the lust of the flesh, and the pride of life (*1 John 2:16*). Examine the temptation and sin of Eve as well as the temptation of

Jesus, and you will find that the temptations for each came from these three categories. Jesus was tempted in every way and in every area that we are, but remained perfectly holy. Although our corrupt natures will have the inner desire to participate in some sins, we have the ability to overcome sin because we are no longer slaves to sin but rather servants of God (*Romans 6*, especially *verses 2 and 16-22*).

∝

24. Question: "Why was Jesus baptized? Why was Jesus' baptism important?"

When Jesus came to John to be baptized, John asked the same question. Why should he, a sinful man, baptize the Messiah? He tried to prevent Jesus from being baptized saying "I need to be baptized by You and You are coming to me?" (*Matthew 3:14*). The baptisms that John performed symbolized repentance, and he saw this as inappropriate for the One he knew to be the spotless Lamb of God. Jesus replied that it should be done because *"it is fitting for us to fulfill all righteousness"* (*Matthew 3:15*). Christ was here identifying Himself with sinners. He will ultimately bear their sins; His perfect righteousness will be imputed to them (*2 Corinthians 5:21*). Therefore, this act of baptism was a necessary part of the righteousness He secured for sinners. His was a perfect righteousness in that He fulfilled all the requirements of the Law which we, for whose sin He would exchange His righteousness, are not capable of fulfilling. He is our perfect substitute.

This baptism was a very public one and was recorded for all generations to know about and understand, and it is important for several reasons. First, it pictures His death and resurrection. Second, it symbolizes the believer's identification with Christ in His death, burial, and resurrection. Third, it marks His first public identification with those whose sins He would bear. Fourth, the event was a public affirmation of His Messiah-ship by the testimony that came directly from heaven (*Matthew 3:17*).

Water baptism is used as a way to identify. In Jesus' day, when a Gentile would convert to Judaism, he would have to be publicly baptized to identify him as a convert. Obviously, Jesus was not converting to anything. Jesus' baptism was an identification of Jesus with the Father and the Holy Spirit. Jesus was baptized to publicly announce Himself as God's Son, and to pronounce the beginning of His ministry with the Holy Spirit's power. Jesus did not "need" the Holy Spirit. However, to set an example for us, Jesus emptied Himself (*Philippians 2:7*) and relied upon the Holy Spirit's power. Jesus' baptism and reliance upon the Holy Spirit is an example that we are to follow in our own lives.

$$\propto$$

25. Question: "Why are Jesus' genealogies in Matthew and Luke so different?"

Jesus' genealogy is given in two places in Scripture, *Matthew chapter 1* and *Luke chapter 3, verses 23-38*. Matthew traces the genealogy from Jesus to Abraham. Luke traces the genealogy from Jesus to Adam. However, there is good reason to believe that Matthew and Luke are in fact tracing entirely different genealogies. For example, Matthew gives Joseph's father as Jacob (*Matthew 1:16*), while Luke gives Joseph's father as Heli (*Luke 3:23*). Matthew traces the line through David's son Solomon (*Matthew 1:6*), while Luke traces the line through David's son Nathan (*Luke 3:31*). In fact, between David and Jesus, the only names the genealogies have in common are Shealtiel and Zerubbabel (*Matthew 1:12; Luke 3:27*). What is the explanation for these differences?

Some point to these differences as evidence of errors in the Bible. However, the Jews were meticulous record keepers, especially in regards to genealogies. It is inconceivable that Matthew and Luke could build two entirely contradictory genealogies of the same lineage. Again, from David through Jesus, the genealogies are completely different. Even the reference to Shealtiel and Zerubbabel likely refer to different individuals of the same names. Matthew gives Shealtiel's father as Jeconiah while Luke gives Shealtiel's father as Neri. It would be normal for a man named Shealtiel to name his son Zerubbabel in light of the famous individuals of those names (see the books of *Ezra* and *Nehemiah*).

Another explanation is that Matthew is tracing the primary lineage while Luke is taking into account the occurrences of "levirite marriage." If a man died without having any sons, it was tradition for the man's brother to marry his wife and have a son who would carry on the man's name. While possible, this view is unlikely as every generation from David to Jesus would have had a "levirite marriage" in order to account for the differences in every generation. This is highly unlikely.

With these concepts in view, most conservative Bible scholars assume Luke is recording Mary's genealogy and Matthew is recording Joseph's. Matthew is following the line of Joseph (Jesus' legal father), through David's son Solomon, while Luke is following the line of Mary (Jesus' blood relative), though David's son Nathan. There was no Greek word for "son-in-law," and Joseph would have been considered a son of Heli through marrying Heli's daughter Mary. Through either line, Jesus is a descendant of David and therefore eligible to be the Messiah. Tracing a genealogy through the mother's side is unusual, but so was the virgin birth. Luke's explanation is that Jesus was the son of Joseph "so it was thought" (*Luke 3:23*).

∞

26. Question: "What does it mean that Jesus is the Son of Man?"

Jesus is referred to as the "Son of Man" 88 times in the New Testament. What does this mean? Does not the Bible say Jesus was the Son of God? How then could Jesus also be the Son of Man? A first meaning of the phrase "Son of Man" is as a reference to the prophecy of *Daniel 7:13-14, "I saw in the night visions, and, behold, one like the Son of man came with the clouds of heaven, and came to the Ancient of days, and they brought Him near before Him. And there was given Him dominion, and glory, and a kingdom, that all people, nations, and languages, should serve Him: His dominion is an everlasting dominion, which shall not pass away, and His kingdom that which shall not be destroyed."* The description "Son of Man" was a Messianic title. Jesus is the one who was given dominion and glory and a kingdom. When Jesus used this phrase related to Himself, He was assigning the "Son of Man" prophecy to Himself. The Jews of that era would have been intimately familiar with the phrase and to whom it referred. He was proclaiming Himself as the Messiah.

A second meaning of the phrase "Son of Man" is that Jesus was truly a human being. God called the prophet Ezekiel "son of man" 93 times. God was simply calling Ezekiel a human being. A son of a man is a man. Jesus was fully God (*John 1:1*), but He was also a human being (*John 1:14*). *1 John 4:2* tells us, *"This is how you can recognize the Spirit of God: Every spirit that acknowledges that Jesus Christ has come in the flesh is from God."* Yes, Jesus was the Son of God, He was in His essence God. Yes, Jesus was also the Son of Man, He was in His essence a human being. In summary, the phrase "Son of Man" indicates that Jesus is the Messiah and that He is truly a human being.

$$\propto$$

27. Question: "What does it mean that Jesus is the Son of God?"

Jesus is not God's Son in the sense of how we think of a father and a son. God did not get married and have a son. Jesus is God's Son in the sense that He is God made manifest in human form (*John 1:1 & 14*). Jesus is God's Son in that He was conceived by the Holy Spirit. *Luke 1:35* declares, *"The angel answered, 'The Holy Spirit will come upon you, and the power of the Most High will overshadow you. So the holy one to be born will be called the Son of God.'"* In Bible times, the phrase "son of man" was used to describe a human being. The son of a man is a man.

During His trial before the Jewish leaders, the High Priest demanded of Jesus, *"I charge you under oath by the living God: Tell us if you are the Christ, the Son of God" (Matthew 26:63).* Jesus responded, *"Yes, it is as you say, 'but I say to all of you: In the future you will see the Son of Man sitting at the right hand of the Mighty One and coming on the clouds of heaven" (Matthew 26:64).* The Jewish leaders responded by accusing Jesus of blasphemy (*Matthew 26:65 & 66*). Later, before Pontius Pilate, *"The Jews insisted, 'We have a law, and according to that law He must die, because He claimed to be the Son of God'" (John 19:7).* Why would claiming to be the "Son of God" be considered blasphemy and be worthy of a death sentence? The Jewish leaders understood exactly what Jesus meant by the phrase "Son of God." To be the "Son of God" is to be of the same nature as God. The "Son of God" is "of God." The claim to be of the same nature as God, to in fact "be

God," was blasphemy to the Jewish leaders; therefore, they demanded Jesus' death. *Hebrews 1:3* expresses this very clearly, *"The Son is the radiance of God's glory and the exact representation of His being...*

Another example can be found in *John 17:12* where Judas is described as the "son of perdition." *John 6:71* tells us that Judas was the son of Simon. What does *John 17:12* mean by describing Judas as the "son of perdition"? The word "perdition" means "destruction, ruin, waste." Judas was not the literal son of "ruin, destruction, and waste" - but those things were the identity of Judas' life. Judas was a manifestation of perdition. In this same aspect, Jesus is the Son of God. The Son of God is God. Jesus is God made manifest (*John 1:1 & 14*).

28. Question: "What does it mean that Jesus is the son of David?"

Seventeen verses in the New Testament describe Jesus as the "son of David." But the question arises, how could Jesus be the son of David if David lived approximately 1000 years before Jesus? The answer is that Christ (the Messiah) was the fulfillment of the prophecy of the seed of David (*2 Samuel 7:14-16*). Jesus was the promised Messiah, which meant He was of the seed of David. *Matthew 1* gives the genealogical proof that Jesus, in His humanity, was a direct descendant of Abraham and David through Joseph, Jesus' legal father. The genealogy in *Luke chapter 3* gives Jesus' lineage through His mother, Mary. Jesus is a descendant of David, by adoption through Joseph, and by blood through Mary. Primarily though, when Christ was referred to as the Son of David, it was meant to refer to His Messianic title as the Old Testament prophesied concerning Him.

Jesus was addressed as "Lord, thou son of David" several times by people who, by faith, were seeking mercy or healing. The woman whose daughter was being tormented by a demon (*Matthew 15:22*), the two blind men by the wayside (*Matthew 20:30*), and blind Bartimaeus (*Mark 10:47*), all cried out to the son of David for help. The titles of honor they gave Him declared their faith in Him. Calling Him Lord expressed their sense of His deity, dominion, and power, and by calling Him "son of David," they were professing Him to be the Messiah.

The Pharisees, too, understood what was meant when they heard the people calling Jesus "son of David." But unlike those who cried out in faith, they were so blinded by their own pride and lack of understanding of the Scriptures that they couldn't see what the blind beggars could see, that here was the Messiah they had supposedly been waiting for all their lives. They hated Jesus because He wouldn't give them the honor they thought they deserved, so when they heard the people hailing Jesus as the Savior, they became enraged (*Matthew 21:15*) and plotted to destroy Him (*Luke 19:47*).

Jesus further confounded the scribes and Pharisees by asking them to explain the meaning of this very title. How could it be that the Messiah is the son of David when David himself refers to Him as "my Lord" (*Mark 12:35-37*)? Of course the teachers of the law couldn't answer the question. Jesus thereby exposed the Jewish spiritual leaders' ineptitude as teachers and their ignorance of what the Old Testament taught as to the true nature of the Messiah, further alienating them from Him.

Jesus Christ, the only son of God and the only means of salvation for the world (*Acts 4:12*), is also the son of David, both in a physical sense and a spiritual sense.

29. Question: "How is Jesus Christ unique?"

⇒ He is the only, unique Son of God (*Psalm 2:7, 11 & 12; John 1:14; Luke 1:35*).

⇒ He is eternal. He existed from eternity past, He exists in the present, and He will exist for all eternity in the future (*John 1:1-3, 14; John 8:58*).

⇒ Jesus alone is the One who bore our sins so that we could have forgiveness and be saved from them (*Isaiah 53; Matthew 1:21; John 1:29; 1 Peter 2:24; 1 Corinthians 15:1-3*).

⇒ Jesus is the only Way to the Father (*John 14:6; Acts 4:12; 1 Timothy 2:5*); there is no other way to salvation. He is the only righteous One who exchanged that perfect righteousness for our sin (*2 Corinthians 5:21*).

⇒ Jesus alone had power over His own death and the ability to take back His life again (*John 2:19; 10:17 & 18*). Note: His resurrection was not a "spiritual" one, but was physical (*Luke 24:39*). His resurrection from the dead, never to die again, distinguished Him as the unique Son of God (*Romans 1:4*).

⇒ Jesus alone accepted worship as an equal with the Father (*John 20:28 & 29; Philippians 2:6*), and indeed God the Father states that the Son is to be honored as He is honored (*John 5:23*). All others, whether Jesus' disciples or angelic beings, rightly reject that worship (*Acts 10:25 & 26; Acts 14:14 & 15; Matthew 4:10; Revelation 19:10; 22:9*).

⇒ Jesus has the power to give life to whom He will (*John 5:21*).

⇒ The Father has committed all judgment to Jesus (*John 5:22*).

⇒ Jesus was with the Father and directly involved in the creation, and it is by His hand that all things are held together (*John 1:1-3; Ephesians 3:9; Hebrews 1:8-10; Colossians 1:17*).

⇒ It is Jesus who will rule the world at the end of this present age (*Hebrews 1:8; Isaiah 9:6 & 7; Daniel 2:35, 44; Revelation 19:11-16*).

⇒ Jesus alone was born of a virgin, conceived by the Holy Spirit (*Isaiah 7:14; Matthew 1:20-23; Luke 1:30-35*).

⇒ It is Jesus who demonstrated that He had the attributes of God [e.g., the power to forgive sins and heal the sick (*Matthew 9:1 -7*); to calm the wind and waves (*Mark 4:37-41; Psalm 89:8 & 9*); to know us, being perfectly acquainted with us (*Psalm 139; John 1:46-50; 2:23-25*), to raise the dead (*John 11; Luke 7:12-15; 8:41-55*), etc.]

⇒ There are a great number of prophecies concerning the Messiah's birth, life, resurrection, person, and purpose. All were fulfilled by Him and no other (*Isaiah 7:14; Micah 5:2; Psalm 22; Zechariah 11:12 & 13; 13:7; Isaiah 9:6 & 7; Isaiah 53; Psalm 16:10*).

30. Question: "What were the seven last words of Jesus Christ on the cross and what do they mean?"

The seven statements that Jesus Christ made on the cross were (not in any particular order):

⇒ *Matthew 27:46* tells us that about the ninth hour Jesus cried with a loud voice, saying, "Eli, Eli, lama sabachthani?" which means, My God, my God, why have you forsaken me? Here, Jesus was expressing His feelings of abandonment as God placed the sins of the world on Him, and because of that, God had to "turn away" from Jesus. As Jesus was feeling that weight of sin, He was experiencing a separation from God for the only time in all of eternity. This was also a fulfillment of the prophetic statement in *Psalm 22:1*.

⇒ "Father, forgive them; for they know not what they do" (*Luke 23:34*). Those who crucified Jesus were not aware of the full scope of what they were doing because they did not recognize Him as the Messiah. While their ignorance of divine truth did not mean they deserved forgiveness, Christ's prayer in the midst of their mocking Him is an expression of the limitless compassion of divine grace.

⇒ "Truly, I say to you, today you will be with me in Paradise" (*Luke 23:43*). In this passage, Jesus is assuring one of the criminals on the cross that when he died, he would be with Jesus in heaven. This was granted because the criminal had expressed his faith in Jesus, recognizing Him for who He was (*Luke 23:42*).

⇒ "Father, into Your hands I commit my spirit" (*Luke 23:46*). Here, Jesus is willingly giving up His soul into the Father's hands, indicating that He was about to die, and that God had accepted His sacrifice. *"He offered up Himself without spot to God" (Hebrews 9:14)*.

⇒ *"Woman, behold your son!"* and *"Behold your mother!"* When Jesus saw His mother standing near the cross with the Apostle John, whom He loved, He committed His mother's care into John's hands. And from that hour John took her unto his own home. (*John 19:26 & 27*). In this verse Jesus, ever the compassionate Son, is making sure His earthly mother is cared for after His death.

⇒ *"I thirst"* (*John 19:28*). Jesus was here fulfilling the

Messianic prophecy from *Psalm 69:21*: *"They gave me poison for food, and for my thirst they gave me vinegar to drink."* By saying He was thirsty, He prompted the Roman guards to give Him vinegar, which was customary at a crucifixion, thereby fulfilling the prophecy.

⇒ *"It is finished!"* (*John 19:30*). Jesus' last words meant that His suffering was over and the whole work His Father had given Him to do, which was to preach the Gospel, work miracles, and obtain eternal salvation for His people, was done, accomplished, fulfilled. The debt of sin was paid.

31. Question: "What was Jesus like as a person?"

Although He had *"no beauty that we should desire Him..."* (*Isaiah 53:2)*, it was His "personality" that drew men to Him. He was a man of great character.

He had a COMPASSIONATE nature. He had compassion on the crowds *"because they were harassed and helpless, like sheep without a shepherd"* (*Matthew 9:36)*. Because of His compassion for them, He healed their diseases (*Matthew 14:14; 20:34*), and because of their hunger, He compassionately created enough food to feed more than 5000 (*Matthew 15:32*).

Jesus was SERIOUS and FOCUSED. He had a mission in life and never got sidetracked from it, knowing the weightiness of it and the shortness of time. His attitude was that of a SERVANT. *"He did not come to BE served, but to SERVE"* (*Mark 10:45)*. KINDNESS and SELFLESSNESS characterized His personality.

Jesus was SUBMISSIVE to His Father's will when He came to earth and subsequently went to the cross. He knew that dying on the cross was the only payment His Father could accept for our salvation. He prayed the night of His betrayal by Judas, *"O My Father, if it be possible, take this cup of suffering from Me: but LET WHAT YOU WANT BE DONE, NOT WHAT I WANT"* (*Matthew 26:39)*. He was a SUBMISSIVE Son to Mary and Joseph, as well. He grew up in a normal (sinful) household, yet, *"He continued in subjection to them..." (Luke 2:51)*. He was OBEDIENT to the Father's will. *"He learned obedience through the things that He suffered" (Hebrews 5:8).* *"For we do not have a high priest who cannot sympathize with our weaknesses, but One who has been tempted in all things as we are, yet without sin" (Hebrews 4:15).*

Jesus had a heart of MERCY and FORGIVENESS - *"Father, forgive them, for they do not know what they are doing" (Luke 23:34). "...If we admit that we have sinned, He will forgive us our sins..." (1 John 1:9).* He was also LOVING in His relationships, *"Now Jesus loved Martha, and her sister, and Lazarus" (John 11:5).* John was known as the disciple *"whom Jesus loved" (John 13:23).*

He had a reputation for being GOOD and CARING. He healed often and in most places where He went IN ORDER THAT they might know who He was! Truly He proved to be the Son of the living God by all the miracles He did, all the while showing concern for the afflictions of those around Him.

HONEST/TRUTHFUL - He never violated His own Word. He spoke TRUTH wherever He went. He lived a life we could follow explicitly. *"I am the WAY, the TRUTH, and the LIFE..." (John 14:6).* At the same time, He was PEACEABLE. He did not argue His case, nor try to bully His way into people's hearts.

Jesus was INTIMATE with His followers. He spent quality and quantity time with them. He coveted their fellowship, taught them, and helped them focus on what was eternal. He was also intimate with His Heavenly Father. He prayed to Him regularly, listened, obeyed, and cared about God's reputation. Angered at the moneychangers who were buying and selling in the temple, He said firmly and AUTHORITA-TIVELY, *"It is written, 'My house shall be called a house of prayer'; but you have made it a robbers den!"* He was obviously a STRONG, but quiet LEADER. Everywhere He went, until the inevitable decline, the people followed Him, eager to listen to His teaching.

He was PATIENT, knowing and understanding our frailties. He was and is *"patient toward you, not wishing for any to perish, but for all to come to repentance" (2 Peter 3:9).*

These are traits that all believers should desire to become a part of their "personality" and character. The things that drew people to Jesus should be the very things that draw people to us. Jesus has given those who believe in Him His Holy Spirit, who enables us to be constantly changing into His image *(Romans 8:29)*. This will only come about as we YIELD to Him for who He truly is...LORD of the universe! We must BELIEVE that He is conforming us into His image, and not resist His will for us. Even as Jesus never drew attention to Himself, (but rather to His Father), even so, we ought to say as John the Baptist did, *"He must increase, but I must decrease" (John 3:30)*.

32. Question: "Was Jesus Christ married?"

No, Jesus Christ was not married. A recent popular book, "The Da Vinci Code," speaks of Christ being married to Mary Magdalene. This myth/lie is absolutely false and has no basis theologically, historically, or Biblically. While a couple of the "Gnostic gospels" mention Jesus having a close relationship with Mary Magdalene, none of them specifically states that Jesus was married to Mary Magdalene, or had any romantic involvement with her. The closest any of them come is saying that Jesus kissed Mary Magdalene, which just as easily could be a reference to a "friendly kiss." Further, even if the Gnostic gospels directly stated that Jesus was married to Mary Magdalene, that would not have any authority, as the Gnostic gospels have all been proven to be forgeries invented to create a Gnostic view of Jesus.

If Jesus had been married, the Bible would have told us so, or there would be some unambiguous statement to that fact. Scripture would not be completely silent on such an important issue. The Bible mentions Jesus' mother, adoptive father, brothers, and sisters. Why would it neglect to even mention the fact that Jesus had a wife? Those who believe/teach that Jesus was married are doing so in an attempt to "humanize" Him, to make Him more ordinary, like everyone else. People simply do not want to believe that Jesus was God in the flesh (*John 1:1, 14; 10:30*). So, they invent and believe myths about Jesus being married, having children, and being an ordinary human being.

A secondary question would be, "Could Jesus Christ have been married?" There is nothing sinful about being married. There is nothing sinful about having sexual relations in marriage. So, yes, Jesus could have been married and still be the sinless Lamb of God, the Savior of the world. At the same time, there is no reason Biblically that Christ would have married. That is not the point in this debate. Those who believe that Jesus was married do not believe that He was sinless, or that He was the Messiah. Getting married and having children is not why God sent Jesus. *Mark 10:45* tells us why Jesus came, *"For even the Son of Man did not come to be served, but to serve, and to give His life as a ransom for many."*

33. Question: "Did Jesus fight Satan for the keys to the kingdom?"

Keys are a symbol of control. Keys keep people in or out. If they do not have a key to a lock, they cannot enter or exit. Keys grant the holder access to interiors and their contents, and in ancient times the wearing of large keys was a mark of status in the community. In the New Testament, the word "Hades" has a twofold usage: in some cases it denotes the place of all the departed dead, the grave in *Acts 2:27 & 31*; in others, it refers to the place of the departed wicked, Hell in *Luke 16:23* and *Revelation 20:13 & 14*. Since Christ alone has conquered death and has Himself come out of grave, He alone can determine who will enter death and Hades and who will come out. He has the "keys." He has authority over death and the place of the dead.

Satan has never possessed these "keys." Satan has never had power to determine who goes to Heaven (the Kingdom) and who goes to Hell. Jesus did not have to fight Satan for the keys because the keys were never in Satan's possession. God and God alone has power over death and Hell (*Revelation 1:18*). Jesus did not have to fight Satan for anything because Jesus' death on the cross was His ultimate victory. *Colossians 2:15* tells us, *"...and having disarmed the powers and authorities, He made a public spectacle of them, triumphing over them by the cross."*

For the Christian, there is no need to fear death and hell. Christ is in control of both, and the one who has faith in Christ will never enter hell. But it must be remembered, ONLY Christ has the keys to the Kingdom. This is why Jesus told us He is the Way, the Truth, and the Life and that NO ONE can come to the Father except by Him (*John 14:6*).

∝

34. Question: "Was Jesus ever angry?"

When Jesus cleared the temple of the moneychangers and animal-sellers, He showed great emotion and anger (*Matthew 21:12 & 13; Mark 11:15-18; John 2:13-22*). Jesus' emotion was described as "zeal" for God's house (*John 2:17*). His anger was pure and completely justified because at its root was concern for God's holiness and worship. Because these were at stake, Jesus took fast and furious action.

Another time Jesus showed anger was in the synagogue of Capernaum. When the Pharisees refused to answer Jesus' questions, *"He . . . looked round about them with anger" (Mark 3:5)*. This verse goes on to give the reason for His anger: *"the hardness of their hearts."*

Many times, we think of anger as a selfish, destructive emotion that we should eradicate from our lives altogether. However, the fact that Jesus did sometimes become angry indicates that anger itself, as an emotion, is not "amoral." This is borne out elsewhere in the New Testament. *Ephesians 4:26* instructs us to *"be angry, and sin not,"* and not to let the sun go down on our anger. The command is not to "avoid anger" (or suppress it or ignore it) but to deal with it properly, in a timely manner. We note the following facts about Jesus' displays of anger:

A. His anger had the proper motivation. In other words, He was angry for the right reasons. Jesus' anger did not arise from petty arguments or personal slights against Him. There was no selfishness involved.

B. His anger had the proper focus. He was not angry at God or at the "weaknesses" of others. His anger targeted sinful behavior and true injustice.

C. His anger had the proper supplement. Mark 3:5 says that His anger was attended by grief over the Pharisees' lack of faith. Jesus' anger stemmed from love for the Pharisees and concern for their spiritual condition. It had nothing to do with hatred or ill will.

D. His anger had the proper control. Jesus was never "out of control," even in His wrath. The temple leaders did not like His cleansing of the temple (Luke 19:47), but He had done nothing amiss. He controlled His emotions; His emotions did not control Him.

E. His anger had the proper duration. He did not allow His anger to turn into bitterness; He did not hold grudges. He dealt with each situation properly, and He handled anger in good time.

F. His anger had the proper result. Jesus' anger had the inevitable consequence of godly action. Jesus' anger, as with all His emotions, was held in check by the Word of God; thus, Jesus' response was always to accomplish God's will.

When we get angry, too often we have improper control or an improper focus. We fail in one or more of the above points. This is the "wrath of man," which *"worketh not the righteousness of God" (James 1:20)*. Jesus did not exhibit the "wrath of man" but the wrath of God.

35. Question: "What is the Jesus Seminar?"

The "Jesus Seminar" was begun by New Testament "scholar" Robert Funk in the 1970s. It was Mr. Funk's desire to rediscover the "historical Jesus" that had been hidden behind almost 2000 years of Christian traditions, myths, and legends. The Jesus Seminar was created to examine the biblical gospels and other early Christian literature to discover who Jesus truly was and what He truly said. The Jesus Seminar was (and still is) comprised primarily of "scholars" who deny the inspiration, authority, and inerrancy of the Bible. The agenda of the Jesus Seminar was not to discover who the historical Jesus was. Rather, the purpose of the Jesus Seminar is to attack what the Bible clearly teaches about whom Jesus is and what He taught.

A recent publication of the Jesus Seminar is a work that goes through the four gospels, and the false gospel of Thomas, and proceeds to determine what Jesus truly said and taught. It divides Jesus' words from the gospels into categories based on how likely it is that Jesus truly said them. Words in red indicate words that Jesus most likely said. Words in pink represent words that Jesus possibly said. Word in grey indicate words that Jesus likely did not say, but are close to what He might have said. Words in black represent words that Jesus definitely did not say. It is interesting to note that in this work from the Jesus Seminar there are more words in black than in red, pink, and grey combined. Almost the entire gospel of John is in black. It is absolutely ridiculous, even offensive, to think that a group of "scholars" today can more accurately determine what Jesus did and did not say than the authors of the gospels, who wrote in the same century in which Jesus lived, taught, died, and was resurrected.

The "scholars" of the Jesus Seminar do not believe in the deity of Christ, the resurrection of Christ, the miracles of Christ, or the substitutionary atonement death of Christ. Perhaps most significant, they deny that the Holy Spirit is the author of all Scripture (*2 Timothy 3:16 & 17*), having moved the minds and hands of all the writers (*2 Peter 1:20 & 21*), and having preserved its message, its meaning and its accuracy down through the centuries. Since the Jesus Seminar does not believe these Christian doctrines, they relegate anything that Jesus is recorded as saying about them as "black." Essentially, the agenda of the Jesus Seminar is, "I do not believe Jesus is God, so I am going to remove anything that records Jesus saying or teaching that He is God from the gospels." The claim that the purpose of the Jesus Seminar is to "discover the historical Jesus" is false and misleading. The true purpose of the Jesus Seminar is to promote the Jesus that the Jesus Seminar believes in instead of the Jesus of the Bible.

36. Question: "Why did Jesus say, 'My God, my God, why have you forsaken me?'?"

"And about the ninth hour Jesus cried with a loud voice, saying, Eli, Eli, lama sabachthani? that is to say, My God, my God, why hast thou

forsaken me?" (Matthew 27:46). This cry is a fulfillment of *Psalm 22:1*, one of many parallels between that psalm and the specific events of the crucifixion. It has been difficult to understand in what sense Jesus was "forsaken" by God. It is certain that God approved His work. It is certain that He was innocent. He had done nothing to forfeit the favor of God. As His own Son; holy, harmless, undefiled, and obedient; God still loved Him. In none of these senses could God have forsaken Him.

However, Isaiah tells us that *"he bore our griefs and carried our sorrows; that he was wounded for our transgressions, and bruised for our iniquities; that the chastisement of our peace was laid upon him; that by his stripes we are healed" (Isaiah 53:4 & 5)*. He redeemed us from the curse of the law, being made a curse for us (*Galatians 3:13*). He was made a sin offering, and He died in our place, on our account, that He might bring us near to God. It was this, doubtless, which caused His intense sufferings. It was the manifestation of God's hatred of sin, in some way which He has not explained, that Jesus experienced in that terrible hour. It was suffering endured by Him that was due to us, and suffering by which, and by which alone, we can be saved from eternal death.

In those awful moments, Jesus was expressing His feelings of abandonment as God placed the sins of the world on Him, and because of that had to "turn away" from Jesus. As Jesus was feeling that weight of sin, He was experiencing separation from God for the only time in all of eternity. It was at this time that *2 Corinthians 5:21* occurred, *"God made Him who had no sin to be sin for us, so that in Him we might become the righteousness of God."* Jesus became sin for us, so He felt the loneliness and abandonment that sin always produces, except that in His case, it was not His sin, it was ours.

37. Question: "If Jesus was God, why did He not know when He would return?"

Speaking of Jesus' Second Coming, *Matthew 24:36* and *Mark 13:32* tell us, *"No one knows about that day or hour, not even the angels in heaven, nor the Son, but only the Father."*

When Jesus spoke these words to the disciples, even He had no knowledge of the date and time of His return. Although Jesus was fully God (*John 1:1, 14*), when He became a man, He voluntarily restricted the use of certain divine attributes (*Philippians 2:6–8*). He did not manifest them unless directed by the Father (*John 4:34; 5:30; 6:38*). He demonstrated His omniscience on several occasions (cf. *John 2:25; 3:13*), but He voluntarily restricted that omniscience to only those things God wanted Him to know during the days of His humanity (*John 15:15*). Such was the case regarding the knowledge of the date and time of His return. After He was resurrected, Jesus resumed His full divine knowledge (cf. *Matthew 28:18; Acts 1:7*).

Matthew 24:36 clearly states that the Father alone knows when Jesus' return will be. Verses such as *John 5:30; 6:38; 8:28 & 29; 10:30; 12:49; 14:28, 31*; and *Matthew 26:39 & 42* demonstrate Jesus' submission to the Father as well as their Oneness in the Godhead. Yes, they are both God. But some things Jesus had apparently chosen to "give up the rights" to be privy to during His earthly ministry (see *Philippians 2:5-11*). Jesus, now exalted in Heaven, surely knows all, including the timing of His Second Coming.

∝

38. Question: "What does it mean that Jesus is the Lamb of God?"

When Jesus is called the Lamb of God in *John 1:29* and *John 1:36*, it is in reference to His being the perfect and ultimate sacrifice for sin. In order to understand who Christ was and what He did, we must begin with the Old Testament, which contains prophecies concerning the coming of Christ as an *"offering for sin"* (*Isaiah 53:10*). In fact, the whole sacrificial system established by God in the Old Testament set the stage for the coming of Jesus Christ, who is the perfect sacrifice that God would provide as atonement for the sins of His people (*Romans 8:3; Hebrews 10*).

The sacrifice of lambs played a very important role in the Jewish religious life and their sacrificial system. When John the Baptist referred to Jesus as the *"Lamb of God who takes away the sin of the world" (John 1:29)*, the Jews who heard him might have immediately thought of any one of several important sacrifices. With the time of the Passover Feast being very near, the first thought might be the sacrifice of the Passover Lamb. The Passover Feast was one of the main Jewish holidays and a celebration in remembrance of when God delivered the Israelites from bondage in Egypt. In fact, the slaying of the Passover Lamb and the applying of the blood to door posts of the houses in order for the death angel to pass over those people who are *"covered by the blood" (Exodus 12:11-13)* is a beautiful picture of Christ's atoning work on the cross.

Another important sacrifice involving lambs was the daily sacrifices at the Temple in Jerusalem. Every morning and evening, a lamb was sacrificed in the Temple for the sins of the people *(Exodus 29:38-42)*. These daily sacrifices, like all others, were simply to point people towards the perfect sacrifice of Christ on the cross. In fact, the time of Jesus' death on the cross corresponds to the time the evening sacrifice would have been being made in the Temple. The Jews at that time would have also been familiar with the Old Testament prophets Jeremiah and Isaiah, whose prophecies foretold the coming of one who would be brought *"like a lamb to the slaughter" (Jeremiah 11:19; Isaiah 53:7)* and whose sufferings and sacrifice would provide redemption for Israel. Of course, that person who was foretold by the Old Testament prophets was none other than Jesus Christ, "the Lamb of God."

While the idea of a sacrificial system might seem strange to us today, the concept of payment or restitution is still one we can easily understand. We know that the wage of sin is death *(Romans 6:23)* and that our sin separates us from God. We also know that the Bible teaches that we are all sinners and that none of us are righteous before God *(Romans 3:23)*. Because of our sin, we are separated from God, and we stand guilty before Him; therefore, the only hope we can have is if He will provide a way for us to be reconciled to Himself and that is what He did in sending His Son Jesus Christ to die on the cross. Christ died to make atonement for sin and to pay the penalty of the sins of all who believe in Him.

It is through His death on the cross as God's perfect sacrifice for sin and His resurrection three days later that we can now have eternal life if we believe in Him. The fact that God Himself has provided the offering that atones or pays for our sin is part of the glorious good news of the gospel that is so clearly declared in *1 Peter 1:18-21* - *"knowing that you were not redeemed with corruptible things, like silver or gold, from your aimless conduct received by tradition from your fathers, but with the precious blood of Christ, as of a lamb without blemish and without spot. He indeed was foreordained before the foundation of the world, but was manifest in these last times for you who through Him believe in God, who raised Him from the dead and gave Him glory, so that your faith and hope are in God."*

$\propto$

39. Question: "What is the kenosis?"

The term kenosis comes from the Greek word for the doctrine of Christ's self-emptying in His incarnation. The kenosis was a self-renunciation, not an emptying Himself of deity nor an exchange of deity for humanity. *Philippians 2:7* tells us that Jesus *"emptied Himself, taking the form of a bond-servant, and being made in the likeness of men."* Jesus did not cease to be God during His earthly ministry. But He did set aside His heavenly glory of a face-to-face relationship with God. He also set aside His independent authority. During His earthly ministry, Christ completely submitted Himself to the will of the Father.

As part of the kenosis, Jesus sometimes operated with the limitations of humanity (*John 4:6; 19:28*). God does not get tired or thirsty. *Matthew 24:36* tells us, *"No one knows about that day or hour, not even the angels in heaven, nor the Son, but only the Father."* We might wonder if Jesus was God, how could He not know everything, as God does (*Psalm 139:1-6*)? It seems that while Jesus was on earth, He surrendered the use of some of His divine attributes. Jesus was still perfectly holy, just, merciful, gracious, righteous, and loving - but to varying degrees Jesus was not omniscient or omnipotent.

However, when it comes to the kenosis, we often focus too much on what Jesus gave up. The kenosis also deals with what Christ took on. Jesus added to Himself a human nature and humbled Himself. Jesus went from being the glory of glories in Heaven to being a human being who was put to death on the cross. *Philippians 2:7 & 8* declares, *"taking the very nature of a servant, being made in human likeness.*

And being found in appearance as a man, He humbled Himself and became obedient to death, even death on a cross!" In the ultimate act of humility, the God of the universe became a human being and died for His creation. The kenosis, therefore, is Christ taking on a human nature with all of its limitations, except with no sin.

40. Question: "What was the meaning and importance of the transfiguration?"

About a week after Jesus plainly told His disciples that He would suffer, be killed, and be raised to life (*Luke 9:22*), He took Peter, James and John up a mountain to pray. While praying, His personal appearance was changed into a glorified form, and His clothing became dazzling white. Moses and Elijah appeared and talked with Jesus about His death that would soon take place. Peter, not knowing what he was saying and being very fearful, offered to put up three shelters for them. This is undoubtedly a reference to the booths that were used to celebrate the Feast of Tabernacles, when the Israelites dwelt in booths for 7 days (*Lev. 23:34–42*). Peter was expressing a wish to stay in that place. When a cloud enveloped them, a voice said, *"This is My Son, whom I have chosen, whom I love; listen to Him!"* The cloud lifted, Moses and Elijah had disappeared, and Jesus was alone with His disciples who were still very much afraid. Jesus warned them not to tell anyone what they had seen until after His resurrection. The three accounts of this event are found in *Matthew 17:1-8, Mark 9:2-8,* and *Luke 9:28-36.*

Undoubtedly, the purpose of the transfiguration of Christ into at least a part of His heavenly glory was so that the "inner circle" of His disciples could gain a greater understanding of who Jesus was. Christ underwent a dramatic change in appearance in order that the disciples could behold Him in His glory. The disciples, who had only known Him in His human body, now had a greater realization of the deity of Christ, though they could not fully comprehend it. That gave them the reassurance they needed after hearing the shocking news of His coming death.

Symbolically, the appearance of Moses and Elijah represented the Law and the Prophets. But God's voice from heaven, *"Listen to Him!"* clearly showed that the Law and the Prophets must give way to Jesus. The One who is the new and living way is replacing the old. He is the fulfillment of the Law and the countless prophecies in the Old Testament. Also, in His glorified form they saw a preview of His coming glorification and enthronement as King of kings and Lord of lords.

The disciples never forgot what happened that day on the mountain and no doubt this was intended. John wrote in his gospel, *"We have seen His glory, the glory of the one and only" (John 1:14)*. Peter also wrote of it, *"We did not follow cleverly invented stories when we told you about the power and coming of our Lord Jesus Christ, but we were eyewitnesses of His majesty. For He received honor and glory from God the Father when the voice came to Him from the Majestic Glory, saying, 'This is my Son, whom I love; with Him I am well pleased.' We ourselves heard this voice that came from heaven when we were with Him on the sacred mountain" (2 Peter 1:16-18)*. Those who witnessed the transfiguration bore witness to it to the other disciples and to countless millions down through the centuries.

$$\propto$$

41. Question: "Why did Jesus command people to not tell others of the miracles He performed?"

After healing a man of leprosy *(Mark 1:41 & 42)*, *"Jesus sent him away at once with a strong warning: 'See that you don't tell this to anyone...'" (Mark 1:43 & 44)*. To our way of thinking, it would seem that Jesus would want everyone to know about the miracle. But Jesus knew that publicity over such miracles might hinder His mission and divert public attention from His message. Mark records that this is exactly what happened. In this man's excitement over his being miraculously healed, he disobeyed. As a result, Christ had to move His ministry away from the city and into the desert regions *(Mark 1:45) "As a result, Jesus could no longer enter a town openly but stayed outside in lonely places. Yet the people still came to Him from everywhere."*

In addition, Christ, though he had cleansed the leper, still required him to be obedient to the law of the land, to go at once to the priest, and not to make delay by stopping to converse about his being healed. It was also possible that, if he did not go at once, evil-minded men would go before him and prejudice the priest, and prevent his declaring the healing to be true because it was done by Jesus. It was of further importance that the priest should pronounce it to be a genuine cure, that there might be no prejudice among the Jews against its being a real miracle.

Finally, Jesus did not want people focusing on the miracles He performed, but rather the message He proclaimed and the death He was going to die. The same is true today. God would rather that we be focused on the healing miracle of salvation through Jesus Christ instead of focusing on other healings and/or miracles.

42. Question: "Was Jesus crucified on a cross, pole, or stake?"

The Bible clearly and undeniably teaches that Jesus died on a cross (*Matthew 27:32, 40 & 42; Mark 15:21, 30 & 32; Luke 23:26; John 19:17, 19, & 25; Acts 2:23; 1 Corinthians 1:17 & 18; Colossians 1:20; 2:14 & 15*). The Greek words in those Scriptures specifically identify a cross, not a pole or stake. The most common method of execution by the Romans in Jesus' time was crucifying a person on a cross, with nails through their hands/wrists and feet/ankles. Sometimes people were tied to the cross in addition to being nailed to it. There were instances where people were crucified to poles, stakes, trees, x-shaped crosses, etc. But this was not the case with Jesus. He was crucified on a cross.

Crucifixion was a form of punishment that had been passed down to the Romans from the Persians, Phoenicians, and Carthaginians. It was designed to be a lingering death. Roman executioners had perfected the art of slow torture while keeping the victim alive. Some victims even lingered until they were eaten alive by birds of prey or wild beasts. Most hung on the cross for days before dying of exhaustion, dehydration, or, most likely, suffocation. When the legs would no longer support the weight of the body, the diaphragm was constricted in a way that made breathing impossible. That is why breaking the legs would hasten death (*John 19:31 & 33*), but this was unnecessary in Jesus' case. The hands were usually nailed through the wrists, and the feet through the instep or the Achilles tendon (sometimes using one nail for both feet). None of these wounds would be fatal, but their pain would become unbearable as the hours dragged on.

The most notable feature of crucifixion was the stigma of disgrace that was attached to it (*Galatians 3:13; 5:11; Hebrews 12:2*). One indignity was the humiliation of carrying one's own cross, which might weigh as much as 200 pounds. The soldiers would escort the prisoner through the crowds to the place of crucifixion. A placard bearing the indictment would be hung around the person's neck. Ultimately, it does not matter what Jesus was crucified on. At the same time, the Bible specifically states that Jesus was crucified on a cross.

43. Question: "What do John 1:1 &14 mean when they declare that Jesus is the Word of God?"

The answer to this question is found by first understanding the reason why John wrote his gospel. We find his purpose clearly stated in *John 20:30-31. "Many other signs therefore Jesus also performed in the presence of the disciples, which are not written in this book; but these have been written that you may believe that Jesus is the Christ, the Son of God; and that believing you may have life in His name."* Once we understand that John's purpose was to introduce the readers of his gospel to Jesus Christ, establishing Who Jesus is (God in the flesh) and what He did, all with the sole aim of leading them to embrace the saving work of Christ in faith, we will be better able to understand why John introduces Jesus as "*The Word*" in *John 1:1.*

By starting out his gospel stating, "*In the beginning was the Word, and the Word was with God, and the Word was God,*" John is introducing Jesus with a word or a term that both his Jewish and Gentile readers would have been familiar with. The Greek word translated "Word" in this passage is Logos, and it was common in both Greek philosophy and Jewish thought of that day. For example, in the Old Testament the "word" of God is often personified as an instrument for the execution of God's will (*Psalm 33:6; 107:20; 119:89; 147:15-18*). So, for his

Jewish readers, by introducing Jesus as the "Word," John is in a sense pointing them back to the Old Testament where the Logos or "Word" of God is associated with the personification of God's revelation. And in Greek philosophy, the term Logos was used to describe the intermediate agency by which God created material things and communicated with them. In the Greek worldview, the Logos was thought of as a bridge between the transcendent God and the material universe. Therefore, for his Greek readers the use of the term Logos would have likely brought forth the idea of a mediating principle between God and the world.

So, essentially, what John is doing by introducing Jesus as the Logos is drawing upon a familiar word and concept that both Jews and Gentiles of his day would have been familiar with and using that as the starting point from which He introduces them to Jesus Christ. But John goes beyond the familiar concept of Logos that his Jewish and Gentile readers would have had and presents Jesus Christ not as a mere mediating principle like the Greeks perceived, but as a personal being, fully divine, yet fully human. Also, Christ was not simply a personification of God's revelation as the Jews thought, but was indeed God's perfect revelation of Himself in the flesh, so much so that John would record Jesus' own words to Philip: *"Jesus said unto Him, 'Have I been so long with you, and yet you have not come to know Me, Philip? He who has seen Me has seen the Father; how do you say, "Show us the Father"?'" (John 14:9)*. By using the term Logos or "Word" in *John 1:1*, John is amplifying and applying a concept that was familiar with his audience and using that to introduce his readers to the true Logos of God in Jesus Christ, the Living Word of God, fully God and yet fully man, who came to reveal God to man and redeem all who believe in Him from their sin.

44. Question: "What is the doctrine of eternal Sonship and is it Biblical?"

The doctrine of eternal Sonship simply affirms that the second Person of the triune Godhead has eternally existed as the Son. In other words, there was never a time when He was not the Son of God, and there has always been a Father/Son relationship within the Godhead. This doctrine recognizes that the idea of Sonship is not merely a title or role that Christ assumed at some specific point in history, but that it is the essential identity of the second Person of the Godhead. According to this doctrine, Christ is and always has been the Son of God.

Yes, the eternal Sonship is biblical and is a view that is widely held among Christians and has been throughout church history. It is important, however, to remember when discussing the doctrine of eternal Sonship that there are evangelical Christians on both sides of this debate. This is not to say that this is not an important doctrine, because it is; it simply acknowledges the fact that there are orthodox or evangelical Christians that hold or have held both views. Those that deny the doctrine of eternal Sonship are not denying the triune nature of God or the deity or eternality of Christ, and those that embrace the eternal Sonship of Christ are not inferring that Jesus Christ was anything less than fully God.

Throughout church history the doctrine of eternal Sonship has been widely held, with most Christians believing that Jesus existed as God's eternal Son before creation. It is affirmed in the Nicene Creed (325 A.D.) which states: "We believe in one God, the Father, the Almighty, maker of heaven and earth, of all that is, seen and unseen. We believe in one Lord, Jesus Christ, the only Son of God, eternally begotten of the Father, God from God, Light from Light, true God from true God, begotten, not made, of one Being with the Father. Through him all things were made. For us and for our salvation he came down from heaven: by the power of the Holy Spirit he became incarnate from the Virgin Mary, and was made man. For our sake he was crucified under Pontius Pilate; he suffered death and was buried. On the third day he rose again in accordance with the Scriptures; he ascended into heaven and is seated at the right hand of the Father. He will come again in glory to judge the living and the dead, and his kingdom will have no end." It was also later reaffirmed in the fifth century in the Athanasian Creed.

There is considerable biblical evidence to support the eternal Sonship of Christ:

⇒ There are many passages that clearly identify that it was "the Son" who created all things (*Colossians 1:13-16; Hebrews 1:2*), thereby strongly implying that Christ was the Son of

God at the time of creation. When one considers these passages, it seems clear that the most normal and natural meaning of the passages is that at the time of creation Jesus was the Son of God, the second Person of the Triune Godhead, thus supporting the doctrine of eternal Sonship.

⇒ There are numerous verses that speak of God the Father sending the Son into the world to redeem sinful man (*John 20:21; Galatians 4:4; 1 John 4:14; 1 John 4:10*) and giving His Son as a sacrifice for sin (*John 3:16*). Clearly implied in all the passages that deal with the Father sending/giving the Son is the fact that He was the Son before He was sent into the world. This is even more clearly seen in *Galatians 4:4-6*, where the term "sent forth" is used both of the Son and the Spirit. Just as the Holy Spirit did not become the Holy Spirit when He was sent to empower the believers at Pentecost, neither did the Son become the Son at the moment of His incarnation. All three Persons of the Triune Godhead have existed for all eternity, and their names reveal who they are, not simply what their title or function is.

⇒ *1 John 3:8* speaks of the appearance or manifestation of the Son of God: *"the one who practices sin is of the devil; for the devil has sinned from the beginning. The Son of God appeared for this purpose, that He might destroy the works of the devil."* The verb "to make manifest" or "appeared" means to make visible or to bring to light something that was previously hidden. The idea communicated in this verse is not that the second Person of the trinity became the Son of God, but that the already existing Son of God was made manifest or appeared in order to fulfill God's predetermined purpose. This idea is also seen in other verses such as *John 11:27* and *1 John 5:20*.

⇒ *Hebrews 13:8* teaches that *"Jesus Christ is the same yesterday and today, yes and forever."* This verse again seems to support the doctrine of eternal Sonship. The fact that Jesus' divine nature is unchanging would seem to indicate that He was always the Son of God because that is an essential part of His Person. At the incarnation Jesus took on human flesh, but His divine nature did not change, nor did His relationship with the Father. This same truth is also implied in *John 20:31*, where we see John's purpose in writing his gospel was so that we might *"believe that Jesus is the Christ, the Son of God;*

and that believing you may have life in His name." It does not say that He became the Son of God but that He is the Son of God. The fact that Jesus was and is the Son of God is an essential aspect of Who He is and His work in redemption.

Finally, one of the strongest evidences for the eternal Sonship of Christ is the triune nature of God and the eternal relationship that exists among the Father, Son, and Holy Spirit. Particularly important is the unique Father/Son relationship that can only be understood from the aspect of Christ's eternal Sonship. This relationship is key to understanding the full measure of God's love for those whom He redeems through the blood of Christ. The fact that God the Father took His Son, the very Son He loved from before the foundation of the world, and sent Him to be a sacrifice for our sins is an amazing act of grace and love that is best understood from the doctrine of eternal Sonship.

One verse that speaks of the eternal relationship between the Father and Son is *John 16:28. "I came forth from the Father, and have come into the world; I am leaving the world again, and going to the Father."* Implied in this verse is again the fact that the Father/Son relationship between God the Father and God the Son is one that always has and always will exist. At His incarnation the Son "came from the Father" in the same sense as upon His resurrection He returned "to the Father." Implied in this verse is the fact that if Jesus was the Son after the resurrection, then He was also the Son prior to His incarnation. Other verses that support the eternal Sonship of Christ would include *John 17:5* and *John 17:24*, which speak of the Father's love for the Son from "before the foundation of the world."

After one considers the many arguments for the doctrine of eternal Sonship, it should become clear that this is indeed a biblical doctrine that finds much support in Scripture. However, that is not to imply that arguments cannot be made against the doctrine as well, or that all Christians will agree to this doctrine. While it has been the view of the majority of Christian commentators throughout history, there have been several prominent Christians on the other side of the issue as well.

Those that deny the doctrine of eternal Sonship would instead hold to a view that is often referred to as the Incarnational Sonship, which teaches that while Christ preexisted, He was not always the Son of God. Those that hold this view believe Christ became the Son of God at some point in history, with the most common view being that Christ became the Son at His incarnation. However, there are others who believe Christ did not become the Son until sometime after His incarnation, such as at His baptism, His resurrection, or His exaltation. It is important to realize that those who deny the eternal Sonship of Christ still recognize and affirm His deity and His eternality.

Those who hold this view see the Sonship of Christ as not being an essential part of Who He is, but instead see it as simply being a role or a title or function that Christ assumed at His incarnation. They also teach that the Father became the Father at the time of the incarnation. Throughout history many conservative Christians have denied the doctrine of eternal Sonship. Some examples would include Ralph Wardlaw, Adam Clarke, Albert Barnes, Finis J. Dake, Walter Martin, and at one time John MacArthur. It is important to note, however, that several years ago John MacArthur changed his position on this doctrine and he now affirms the doctrine of eternal Sonship.

One of the verses commonly used to support Incarnational Sonship is *Hebrews 1:5*, which appears to speak of God the Father's begetting of God the Son as an event that takes place at a specific point in time: *"Thou art My Son, Today I have begotten Thee. And again. I will be a Father to Him. And He shall be a Son to Me."* Those who hold to the doctrine of Incarnational Sonship point out two important aspects of this verse.

⇒ that "begetting" normally speaks of a person's origin, and
⇒ that a Son is normally subordinate to his father.

They reject the doctrine of eternal Sonship in an attempt to preserve the perfect equality and eternality of the Persons of the Triune Godhead. In order to do so, they must conclude that "Son" is simply a title or function that Christ took on at His incarnation and that "Sonship" refers to the voluntary submission that Christ to the Father at His incarnation (*Philemon 2:5-8; John 5:19*).

Some of the problems with the Incarnational Sonship of Christ are that this teaching confuses or destroys the internal relationships that exist within the Trinity, because if the Son is not eternally begotten by the Father, then neither did the Spirit eternally proceed from the Father through the Son. Also, if there is no Son prior to the incarnation, then there is no Father either; and yet throughout the Old Testament we see

God being referred to as the Father of Israel. Instead of having a triune God eternally existing in three distinct Persons with three distinct names, Father, Son, and Holy Spirit, those who hold to the doctrine of *in*carnational Sonship end up with a nameless Trinity prior to the incarnation, and we would be forced to say that God has chosen not to reveal Himself as He truly is, but only as He was to become. In other words, instead of actually revealing who He is, the Triune God instead chose to reveal Himself by the titles He would assume or the roles that He would take on and not who He really is. This is dangerously close to modalism and could easily lead to false teachings about the nature of God. One of the weaknesses of the doctrine of Incarnational Sonship is that the basic relationships existing among the members of the Trinity are confused and diminished. Taken to its logical conclusion, denying the eternal Sonship of Christ reduces the Trinity from the relationship of Father, Son, and Holy Spirit to simply Number One, Number Two and Number Three Persons—with the numbers themselves being an arbitrary designation, destroying the God-given order and relationship that exists among the Persons of the Trinity.

45. Question: "If His name was Yeshua, why do we call Him Jesus?"

Yeshua is the Hebrew name, and its English spelling is Joshua. Iesous is the Greek transliteration of the Hebrew name, and its English spelling is "Jesus." Thus, the names Joshua and Jesus are essentially the same; both are English pronunciations of the Hebrew and Greek names for the Lord. (For examples of how the two names are interchangeable, see *Acts 7:45* and *Hebrews 4:8* in the KJV. In both cases, the word Jesus refers to the Old Testament character Joshua.)

In German, our English word "book" is buch. In Spanish, it becomes a libro; in French, a livre. The language changes, but the object itself does not. In the same way, we can refer to Jesus as "Jesus," "Yeshua," or "YehSou" (Cantonese), without changing His nature. In any language, His name means "the Lord Is Salvation."

We refer to Him as "Jesus" because, as English-speaking people, we know of Him through English translations of the Greek New Testament. Scripture does not value one language over another, and it gives no indication that we must resort to Hebrew when addressing the Lord.

The command is to *"call on the name of the Lord,"* with the promise that we *"shall be saved" (Acts 2:21; Joel 2:32).* Whether we call on Him in English, Korean, Hindi, or Hebrew, the result is the same: the Lord is salvation.

46. Question: "Why wasn't Jesus named Immanuel?"

In the prophecy of the virgin birth, *Isaiah 7:14*, the prophet Isaiah declared, *"Therefore the Lord Himself will give you a sign: The virgin will be with child and will give birth to a son, and will call Him Immanuel."* This prophecy refers to the birth of Jesus in *Matthew 1:22-23, "All this took place to fulfill what the Lord had said through the prophet: 'The virgin will be with child and will give birth to a son, and they will call him Immanuel' which means, 'God with us.'"* This does not mean, however, that the Messiah's name would actually be Immanuel.

There are many names given to Jesus using the phrase "He shall be called," both in the Old and New Testaments. This was a common way of saying that people would refer to Him in these various ways. Isaiah prophesied of the Messiah, *"His name shall be called Wonderful, Counselor, The mighty God, The everlasting Father, The Prince of Peace" (Isaiah 9:6).* None of these titles were Jesus' actual name, but these were descriptions people would use to refer to Him forever. Luke tells us Jesus *"shall be called the Son of the Highest" (Luke 1:32)* and *"son of God" (1:35)* and *"the prophet of the Highest" (1:76),* but none of these were His name.

In two different places, the prophet Jeremiah says in referring to the coming Messiah, *"And this is His name by which He shall be called, JEHOVAH, OUR RIGHTEOUSNESS" (Jeremiah 23:5 & 6; 33:15 & 16).* Now we know that God, the Father, is named Jehovah. Jesus was never actually called Jehovah as though it was His name, but His role was that of bringing the righteousness of Jehovah to those who would believe in Him, exchanging that righteousness for our sin (*2 Corinthians 5:21*). Therefore, this is one of the many titles or "names" which belong to Him.

In the same way, to say that Jesus would be called "Immanuel" means Jesus is God and that He dwelt among us in His incarnation and that He is always with us. Jesus was God in the flesh. Jesus was God making His dwelling among us *(John 1:1 & 14)*. No, Jesus' name was not Immanuel, but Jesus was the meaning of Immanuel, "God with us." Immanuel is one of the many titles for Jesus, a description of who He is.

⊂✕

47. Question: "The Jesus Papers - what are they?"

In 2006, author Michael Baigent released a book entitled, "The Jesus Papers." The subtitle of the book is "Exposing the Greatest Cover-Up in History." The supposed cover-up exposed by "The Jesus Papers" is that Jesus survived the crucifixion and was alive as late as A.D. 45. The "Jesus Papers" themselves are documents that "prove" the conspiracy theory, including documents supposedly written by Jesus Himself.

The gist of the book is that Jesus and Pontius Pilate made a secret agreement that Jesus would not be killed, but rather would be crucified and then rescued. Pilate did not want to crucify Jesus, likely the only concept in which "The Jesus Papers" and the biblical gospels agree. However, Pilate was under great pressure to please the Jewish authorities and prevent a riot. So, during one of the private discussions between Jesus and Pilate, they arranged the scheme. Further biblical evidence of this conspiracy, according to "The Jesus Papers," is the fact that Jesus "died" so quickly, and that Pilate allowed Jesus' body to be removed from the cross after only a few hours.

⇒ There are many, many problems with this conspiracy theory:
⇒ It is highly unlikely that anyone could survive crucifixion. While the historian Josephus records a friend of his surviving crucifixion, the odds would be astoundingly low.

⇒ Each of the four biblical gospels specifically records Jesus' death, burial, and resurrection three days later. Jesus *"gave up His spirit" (John 19:30; Luke 23:46)*.

⇒ If Jesus had survived the crucifixion, the disciples would have clearly seen that Jesus had not been resurrected. The wounds of crucifixion would have rendered Jesus crippled for months. Why would the disciples all be willing to die horrendous deaths for a belief in Jesus' resurrection, which they all knew to be a lie?

⇒ Why would Pontius Pilate, a brutal Roman governor, be willing to negotiate a deal with a "trouble-maker" from Galilee? Pilate ordered the torture and crucifixion of hundreds of people. He would have had no good reason to spare Jesus' life.

Like most conspiracy theories, "The Jesus Papers" is high on conspiracy and low on evidence. Even the author admits that it is an improbable theory. Further, the author admits that neither he, nor anyone else, has ever actually seen the supposed document that proves Jesus survived the crucifixion. There is absolutely not even a shred of evidence for "The Jesus Papers" theory, whether in the Bible, or in history. The real issue here is the authority of Scripture. The Bible is the very Word of God, given by inspiration of the Holy Spirit to the men who penned it *(2 Timothy 3:16)*. Its prophecies, histories and science are 100% accurate, and its authenticity has been miraculously preserved through countless translations over thousands of years. Most of all, unlike frauds (i.e.The Jesus Papers and The DaVinci Code), the power of God to transform lives in its pages. God's extraordinary plan for the salvation of mankind is the central theme of His book. Jesus died on the cross, as the atoning sacrifice for our sins, just as the Bible says He did *(1 John 2:2)*.

∝

48. Question: "Is it wrong to have pictures of Jesus?"

When trying to decide what, if any, Christian imagery is appropriate to place in our homes, a good place to begin is the Ten Commandments. When God first gave His law to mankind, He began with Himself, a statement of who He is: *"the Lord your God, who brought you out of Egypt" (Exodus 20:2)*, and a warning that we are to have no other God but Him. He immediately followed that by forbidding the making of any image of anything *"in heaven above or on earth beneath or in the waters below" (Exodus 20:4)*, for the purpose of worshipping or bowing down to it. The fascinating thing about the history of the Jewish people is that they disobeyed this commandment more than any other. Again and again, they made idols to represent God and worshipped them, beginning with the creation of the golden calf at the very moment God was writing the Ten Commandments on tablets for Moses (*Exodus 32*)! Idol worship not only drew the Israelites away from the true and living God, it led to all manner of sins including temple prostitution and orgies, and even the sacrificing of children to these false gods.

The God who created us, and who knows how deeply we are affected by sin, understands our desire to condense Him into a form we can see and understand. Perhaps it is the fact that our limited minds simply cannot comprehend that which is infinite and eternal. Or, more likely, perhaps we are simply more comfortable when we can reduce God to a more manageable form, such as a picture or a statue. Man has always attempted to humanize God, to make Him over in our own image and bring Him down to our level. After all, if God is just like us, it stands to reason that we are just like Him, a very appealing concept (certainly popular today) and the same lie Satan has been feeding us since the Garden of Eden when he tempted Eve to eat of the forbidden tree: *"You shall be like God" (Genesis 3:5)*.

Just as making idols led the Israelites away from the true worship of God, hanging a portrait of Jesus in our homes would seem to present a continual temptation to reduce Him to nothing more than the image in the picture. Even if we are not bowing down and worshipping the picture, how can we not eventually equate Him in our minds with this simple image? How can we look at it every day and not be tempted to see Him as merely the figure in the picture? But can we possibly reduce Christ's nature, character and power to a two-dimensional, eight-by-ten portrait? In addition, most of the "portraits" of Jesus portray Him in a softened, quasi-romantic style as a handsome and winsome young man while, in fact, He *"had no beauty or majesty to attract us to him, nothing in his appearance that we should desire him" (Isaiah 53:2)*. If it were important for us to know what He really did look like, Matthew, Peter and John, who spent three years with Him, would certainly be able to give us an accurate description, as would His own brother, Jude. Yet, these New Testament writers offer no details about His physical attributes. Does this not suggest that, inspired by the Holy Spirit, they did so in order to carefully avoid encouraging us to make any image of Him?

We certainly don't need a picture to display to us the nature of our Lord and Savior. We have only to look at the creation, as we are reminded in *Psalm 19:1-2: "The heavens declare the glory of God; and the expanse proclaims His handiwork. Day to day pours forth speech, and night to night reveals knowledge."* In addition, our very existence as the redeemed of the Lord, sanctified and made righteous by His blood, shed on the cross for our sins, should have Him always before our eyes and minds.

The Bible, the very Word of God, is also filled with images of Christ that capture our imaginations and thrill our souls. He is the Light of the world (*John 1:4-5*); the very Bread of life (*John 6:32-33*); the living Water that quenches the thirst of our souls (*John 4:14*); the High Priest who intercedes for us with the Father (*Hebrews 2:17*); the Good Shepherd who lays down His life for us, His sheep (*John 10:11 & 14*); the spotless Lamb of God slain before the foundation of the world (*Revelation 13:8*), the Author and Perfecter of our faith (*Hebrews 12:2*); the Way, the Truth, the Life (*John 14:6*); and the very image of the invisible God (*Colossians 1:15*). How can we even consider reducing Him to a piece of paper and hanging Him on the wall?

$\propto$

49. Question: "Is Isaiah 53 'The Suffering Servant' a prophecy about Jesus?"

Perhaps the greatest of all Messianic prophecies in the Tanakh (the Hebrew Scriptures/the Old Testament) concerning the advent of the Jewish Messiah is found in the *53rd chapter* of the prophet *Isaiah*. This section of the Prophets, also known as the "Suffering Servant," has been long understood by the historical Rabbis of Judaism to speak of the Redeemer who will one day come to Zion. Here is a sampling of what Judaism has traditionally believed about the identity of the

"Suffering Servant" of *Isaiah 53*:

⇒ The Babylonian Talmud says: "The Messiah, what is his name? The Rabbis say, The Leper Scholar, as it is said, 'surely he has borne our griefs and carried our sorrows: yet we did esteem him a leper, smitten of God and afflicted...'" (Sanhedrin 98b).

⇒ Midrash Ruth Rabbah says: "Another explanation (of *Ruth 2:14*): He is speaking of king Messiah; 'Come hither,' draw near to the throne; 'and eat of the bread,' that is, the bread of the kingdom; 'and dip thy morsel in the vinegar,' this refers to his chastisements, as it is said, 'But he was wounded for our transgressions, bruised for our iniquities.'"

⇒ The Targum Jonathan says: "Behold my servant Messiah shall prosper; he shall be high and increase and be exceedingly strong."

⇒ The Zohar says: "'He was wounded for our transgressions,' etc....There is in the Garden of Eden a palace called the Palace of the Sons of Sickness; this palace the Messiah then enters, and summons every sickness, every pain, and every chastisement of Israel; they all come and rest upon him. And were it not that he had thus lightened them off Israel and taken them upon himself, there had been no man able to bear Israel's chastisements for the transgression of the law: and this is that which is written, 'Surely our sicknesses he hath carried.'"

⇒ The great (Rambam) Rabbi Moses Maimonides says: "What is the manner of Messiah's advent....there shall rise up one of whom none have known before, and signs and wonders which they shall see performed by him will be the proofs of his true origin; for the Almighty, where he declares to us his mind upon this matter, says, 'Behold a man whose name is the Branch, and he shall branch forth out of his place' (Zechariah 6:12). And Isaiah speaks similarly of the time when he shall appear, without father or mother or family being known, He came up as a sucker before him, and as a root out of dry earth, etc....in the words of Isaiah, when describing the manner in which kings will harken to him, *"At him kings will shut their mouth; for that which had not been told them have they seen, and that which they had not heard they have perceived"*

⇒ Unfortunately, modern Rabbis of Judaism believe that the "Suffering Servant" of *Isaiah 53* refers perhaps to Israel, or to Isaiah himself, or even Moses or another of the Jewish prophets. But Isaiah is clear - he speaks of the Messiah, as many ancient rabbis concluded.

⇒ The *second verse of Isaiah 53* confirms this clarity. The figure grows up as *"a young plant, and like a root out of dry ground."* The shoot springing up is beyond reasonable doubt a reference to the Messiah, and, in fact, it is a common Messianic reference in Isaiah and elsewhere. The Davidic dynasty was to be cut down in judgment like a felled tree, but it was promised to Israel that a new sprout would shoot up from the stump. King Messiah was to be that sprout.

⇒ Beyond doubt, the "Suffering Servant" of *Isaiah 53* refers to Messiah. He is the one highly exalted before whom kings shut their mouths. Messiah is the shoot who sprung up from the fallen Davidic dynasty. He became the King of Kings. He provided the ultimate atonement.

⇒ *Isaiah 53* must be understood as referring to the coming Davidic King, the Messiah. King Messiah was prophesied to suffer and die to pay for our sins and then rise again. He would serve as a priest to the nations of the world and apply the blood of atonement to cleanse those who believe. There is One alone to whom this can refer, Jesus Christ!

⇒ Those who confess him are his children, his promised offspring, and the spoils of his victory. According to the testimony of the Jewish Apostles, Jesus died for our sins, rose again, ascended to the right hand of God, and he now serves as our great High Priest who cleanses us of sin (*Hebrew 2:17; 8:1*). Jesus, the Jewish Messiah, is the one Isaiah foresaw.

⇒ Rabbi Moshe Kohen Ibn Crispin said, "This rabbi described those who interpret *Isaiah 53* as referring to Israel as those "having forsaken the knowledge of our Teachers, and inclined after the `stubbornness of their own hearts,' and of their own opinion, I am pleased to interpret it, in accordance with the teaching of our Rabbis, of the King Messiah. This prophecy was delivered by Isaiah at the divine command for the purpose of making known to us something about the nature of the future Messiah, who is to come and deliver Israel, and his life from the day when he arrives at discretion until his advent as a redeemer, in order that if anyone should arise claiming to be himself the Messiah, we may reflect, and look to see whether we can observe in him any resemblance to the traits described here; if there is any such resemblance, then we may believe that he is the Messiah our righteousness; but if not, we cannot do so."

50. Question: "What is the Swoon Theory? Did Jesus survive the crucifixion?"

The Swoon Theory is the belief that Jesus didn't really die at His crucifixion, but was merely unconscious when He was laid in the tomb and there He resuscitated. Accordingly, His appearances after three days in the tomb were merely perceived to be resurrection appearances. There are several reasons why this theory is invalid and can be easily proven as false, and there were at least three different persons or groups involved in Jesus' crucifixion who were all satisfied concerning the fact of His death on the cross. They are the Roman guards, Pilate, and the Sanhedrin.

⇒ **The Roman Guards** - There were two separate groups of Roman soldiers given the task of ensuring the death of Jesus: the executioners and the tomb guards. The soldiers in charge of execution were specialists in capital punishment, and crucifixion was one of the most brutal forms of execution in history. Jesus was nailed to a cross after enduring horrible beatings at the hands of these professional death merchants, and every person put to death by way of crucifixion was dealt with by these soldiers. Their job was to ensure the task was completed. Jesus could not have survived crucifixion and these soldiers made certain that Jesus was dead before His body was allowed to be taken from the cross. They were completely satisfied that Jesus was truly dead. The second group of soldiers was given the task of guarding the tomb of Jesus because of the request made to Pilate by the Sanhedrin. *Matthew 27:62-66 tells us "On the next day, which followed the Day of Preparation, the chief priests and Pharisees gathered together to Pilate, saying, 'Sir, we remember, while He was still alive, how that deceiver said, "After three days I will rise." Therefore command that the tomb be made secure until the third day, lest His disciples come by night and steal Him away, and say to the people, "He has risen from the dead." So the last deception will be worse than the first.' Pilate said to them, 'You have a guard; go your way, make it as secure as you know how.' So they went and made the tomb secure, sealing the stone and setting the guard"* (NKJV). These guards ensured that the tomb was secure, and their lives depended upon completion of their mission. Only the resurrection of the Son of God could have stayed them from their task.

⇒ **Pilate** - Pilate gave the order for Jesus to be crucified and entrusted this task to be carried out by a Roman centurion, a trusted and proven commander of 100 Roman soldiers. After the crucifixion, a request for the body of Jesus was made by Joseph of Arimathea, in order that His body could be placed in a tomb. Only after confirmation was given to him by his centurion did Pilate release the body into the care of Joseph. *Mark 15:42-45: "Now when evening had come, because it was the Preparation Day, that is, the day before the Sabbath, Joseph of Arimathea, a prominent council member, who was himself waiting for the kingdom of God, coming and taking courage, went in to Pilate and asked for the body of Jesus. Pilate marveled that He was already dead; and summoning the centurion, he asked him if He had been dead for some time. And when he found out from the centurion, he granted the body to Joseph"* (NKJV). Pilate was completely satisfied that Jesus was truly dead.

⇒ **The Sanhedrin** - The Sanhedrin was the ruling council of the Jewish people, and they requested that the bodies of those crucified, including Jesus, be taken down from the cross after their death because of the ensuing Sabbath day. *John 19:31-37: "Therefore, because it was the Preparation Day, that the bodies should not remain on the cross on the Sabbath (for that Sabbath was a high day), the Jews asked Pilate that their legs might be broken, and that they might be taken away. Then the soldiers came and broke the legs of the first and of the other who was crucified with Him. But when they came to Jesus and saw that He was already dead, they did not break His legs. But one of the soldiers pierced His side with a spear, and immediately blood and water came out. And he who has seen has testified, and his testimony is true; and he knows that he is telling the truth, so that you may believe. For these things were done that the Scripture should be fulfilled, 'Not one of His bones shall be broken.' And again another Scripture says, 'They shall look on Him whom they pierced.'"* These Jews who demanded that Jesus be crucified, and even going so far as to suggest an insurrection had He not been crucified, would never have allowed Jesus' body to be removed from the cross were He not already dead. These men were completely satisfied that Jesus was truly dead.

There is other evidence that the Swoon Theory is invalid, such as the condition of Jesus' body after the resurrection. At every appearance, Jesus' body was shown to be in a glorified state, and the only marks remaining as proof of His crucifixion were the nail prints He asked Thomas to touch as proof of Who He was. Anyone who had experienced what Jesus experienced would have needed months to recover physically. Jesus' body bore only the marks of the nails in His hands and feet. The way in which Jesus' body was prepared after the crucifixion is further evidence to refute the theory. Had Jesus only been unconscious, the linens He was wrapped in would have been impossible for Him to escape from, had He been merely a man. The way in which the women attended to Jesus' body is further evidence of his death. They came to the tomb on the first day of the week to further anoint His body with embalming ointments as they had little time to prepare His body prior to the beginning of the Sabbath after His crucifixion. Had He been merely unconscious as the theory supposes, they would have brought medicinal tools to help in His resuscitation.

The purpose for the Swoon Theory is not to dispute His death, but rather, it seeks to disprove His resurrection. If Jesus didn't resurrect, then He's not God. If Jesus truly died and rose from the dead, His power over death proves that He is the Son of God. The evidence demands the verdict: Jesus truly died on the cross, and Jesus truly rose from the dead.

51. Question: "Why did Jesus teach in parables?"

It has been said that a parable is an earthly story with a heavenly meaning. The Lord Jesus frequently used parables as a means of illustrating profound, divine truths. Stories such as these are easily remembered. The characters are bold and the symbolism rich in meaning. Parables were a common form of teaching in Judaism. Before a certain point in His ministry, Jesus had employed many graphic analogies using common things that would be familiar to everyone (salt, bread, sheep, etc.) and their meaning was fairly clear in the context of His teaching. Parables required more explanation, and at one point in His ministry, Jesus began to teach using parables exclusively.

The question is why Jesus would let most people wonder about the meaning of His parables. The first instance of this is in His telling the parable of the seed and the soils. Before He interpreted this parable, He drew His disciples away from the crowd. They said to Him, *"Why do You speak to them in parables?" Jesus answered them, "To you it has been granted to know the mysteries of the kingdom of heaven, but to them it has not been granted. For whoever has, to him more shall be given, and he will have an abundance; but whoever does not have, even what he has shall be taken away from him. Therefore I speak to them in parables; because while seeing they do not see, and while hearing they do not hear, nor do they understand. In their case the prophecy of Isaiah is being fulfilled, which says, 'Hearing you will hear and shall not understand, And seeing you will see and not perceive; For the hearts of this people have grown dull. Their ears are hard of hearing, And their eyes they have closed, Lest they should see with their eyes and hear with their ears, Lest they should understand with their hearts and turn, So that I should heal them.' But blessed are your eyes, because they see; and your ears, because they hear. For truly I say to you that many prophets and righteous men desired to see what you see, and did not see it, and to hear what you hear, and did not hear it" (Matthew 13:10-17).*

Here Matthew seems to suggest that their own unbelief is the cause of their spiritual blindness. The same event as told by Luke, however, emphasizes God's initiative in obscuring the truth from these unbelievers, *"to the rest it is given in parables, [so] that 'Seeing they may not see, And hearing they may not understand'" Luke 8:10.* Both things are true, of course. Yet we are not to think that God blinds them because He somehow delights in their destruction. This judicial blinding may be viewed as an act of mercy, lest their condemnation be increased. He employed parables to obscure the truth from unbelievers while making it clearer to His disciples. For the remainder of His Galilean ministry, He did not speak to the multitudes except in parables (*v. 34*). Jesus' veiling the truth from unbelievers this way was both an act of judgment and an act of mercy. It was judgment because it kept them in the darkness that they loved (*John 3:19*), but it was mercy because they had already rejected the light, so any exposure to more truth would only increase their condemnation.

Our Lord Jesus understood that truth is not sweet music to all ears. Simply put, there are those who have neither interest nor regard in the deep things of God. So why, then, did He speak in parables? To those with a genuine hunger for God, the parable is both an effective and memorable vehicle for the conveyance of divine truths. Our Lord's parables contain great volumes of truth in very few words, and His parables, rich in imagery, are not easily forgotten. So, then, the parable is a blessing to those with willing ears. But to those with dull hearts and ears that are slow to hear, the parable is also an instrument of both judgment and mercy.

52. Question: "What does INRI stand for? What was written on the sign nailed to the cross above Jesus' head?"

John 19:19 records, *"Pilate had a notice prepared and fastened to the cross. It read: JESUS OF NAZARETH, THE KING OF THE JEWS." John 19:20* continues, *"Many of the Jews read this sign, for the place where Jesus was crucified was near the city, and the sign was written in Aramaic, Latin and Greek."* Today, many times when the cross of Jesus is displayed, the letters INRI are placed on the sign above the cross. In Latin, the text "JESUS OF NAZARETH, THE KING OF THE JEWS" would have been written, "Iesus Nazarenus Rex Iudaeorum." Abbreviating this phrase results in "INRI." It is unlikely that the letters INRI were truly on the sign that Pilate placed over Jesus' head, as *John 19:20* specifically states that the sign was written in Aramaic, Greek, and Latin.

Although John's gospel refers to the writing as a "title," Mark and Matthew both refer to it as an "accusation." It was customary to set up over the heads of persons crucified the crime for which they suffered, and the name of the sufferer. The accusation on which Jesus had been condemned by Pilate was his claiming to be the King of the Jews. Ironically, the "crime" for which Jesus was crucified is not a crime at all, but an absolutely true statement. Not only is Jesus King of the Jews, He is the King of all. He is the King of kings and the Lord of lords (*Revelation 17:14* and *19:16*). He is King over the entire universe and all its inhabitants. And it was not any crime of His own that was nailed to the cross; it was the crimes (sins) of everyone who would ever put his or her faith in Him for salvation. He has *"blotted out the handwriting of ordinances that was against us, which was contrary to us, and has taken it out of the way, nailing it to the cross" (Colossians 2:14).*

Just as the title King of the Jews was written in three languages, so do those of all nations and languages recognize Him as Savior, as indeed He is of all the elect of God whom He saves from all their sins, by bearing them in His own body on the cross, and of whom He is the able and willing, the perfect and complete, the only and everlasting Savior.

53. Question: "How long was Jesus' ministry?"

According to *Luke 3:1*, John the Baptist began his ministry in the 15th year of Tiberius' reign (29 AD). Jesus began His ministry shortly thereafter at the age of thirty *(Luke 3:23)*. Incidentally, this indicates that Jesus was probably born around 1 BC (please note: there was no year zero – 1 AD immediately followed 1 BC). This contradicts the popular date of 4 BC for Herod the Great's death since Jesus was born while Herod was still alive. Recent scholarship, however, has discredited the popular view in favor of 1 BC; or more specifically, sometime between the January 9th lunar eclipse of 1 BC and the Feast of Passover a few months later. This tentatively corroborates Luke's account.

Regardless of the questions surrounding the date of Herod's death, the dates of Tiberius' reign have been confidently established. They give us a firm basis upon which we can approximate what year Jesus began His public ministry: around 29 AD. As for the end of His ministry, we know that it culminated with His crucifixion, resurrection and ascension.

According to the Gospel accounts, Christ was crucified the day before Passover, was *"three days and three nights in the heart of the earth" (Matthew 12:38-40)*, and was resurrected before sunrise on a Sunday. In order for Christ to have been crucified the day before Passover and resurrected on a Sunday three days and three nights later, Passover would have had to fall on a Friday, whereby Christ was crucified on a Thursday.

For example, Passover of 30 AD fell on a Thursday (April 6th). To be crucified the day before Passover (Wednesday) and resurrected on Sunday, Jesus would have been in the grave Wednesday afternoon, Wednesday night, Thursday day, Thursday night, Friday day, Friday night, Saturday day, Saturday night, Sunday morning before sunrise. That is four nights – one too many. So 30 AD doesn't work. Plus, according to John's Gospel, Jesus attended at least three annual Feasts of Passover throughout the course of His ministry: one in *John 2:23*, another in *6:4* and the Passover of His crucifixion in *11:55-57*. So one year (29 to 30 AD) just isn't enough time.

Based on the dates provided by Sir Robert Anderson in his The Coming Prince (Kregel: Grand Rapids, p. 104), we used the Rosetta Calendar online calendar conversion service to establish which days of the week Passover fell upon between the years 29 AD (our starting point) and 37 AD. Here are Anderson's dates and their respective days of the week (please note that these are Julian rather than Gregorian dates):

⇒ Passover of 29 AD fell on a Sunday (April 17th)
⇒ Passover of 30 AD fell on a Thursday (April 6th)
⇒ Passover of 31 AD fell on a Tuesday (March 27th)
⇒ Passover of 32 AD fell on a Monday (April 14th)
⇒ Passover of 33 AD fell on a Friday (April 3rd)
⇒ Passover of 34 AD fell on a Tuesday (March 23rd)
⇒ Passover of 35 AD fell on a Monday (April 11th)
⇒ Passover of 36 AD fell on a Friday (March 30th)
⇒ Passover of 37 AD fell on a Thursday (April 18th)

Using this range of dates and assuming that Christ was in the grave for three days and three nights and resurrected on Sunday, we can narrow down the year of Christ's crucifixion to one of two possibilities: 33 or 36 AD. A prophecy from the book of *Daniel* seems to favor the earlier date of 33 AD.

In *Daniel 9*, Gabriel tells Daniel that *"Seventy sevens have been decreed for your people... From the issuing of a decree to restore and rebuild Jerusalem until Messiah the Prince, there will be seven sevens and sixty-two sevens; it will be built again, with plaza and moat, even in times of distress. Then after the sixty-two weeks the Messiah will be cut off and have nothing, and the people of the prince who is to come will destroy the city and the sanctuary and its end will come with a flood; even to the end there will be war; desolations are determined." (9:24-26)*

Seven sevens + 62 sevens = 69 sevens. 69 seven-year periods would pass from the decree to rebuild Jerusalem until the coming of the Messiah. The Messiah would be "cut off" and the city and temple would be destroyed again. A 70th seven-year period would follow.

While the prophecy does not specify what the sevens are, the immediate context implies that they are years. Daniel's prayer in *verses 3-19* focuses on the fulfillment of a 70 year period – the 70 years of Babylonian captivity as prophesied by *Jeremiah (25:11)*. The 70 sevens prophecy was delivered to him in response to this prayer. 70 years fulfilled; 7 times 70 still to come.

Scholars generally agree that this prophecy is according to the ancient 360-day calendar employed by both the Hebrews and the Babylonians (Daniel being written in Babylon during the Babylonian captivity after the fall and decimation of Jerusalem by King Nebuchadnezzar). 69 x 7 years = 483 years. 483 years x 360 days = 173,880 days.

Persian Emperor Artaxerxes Longimanus (who ruled Persia from 464-424 BC) issued the edict to rebuild Jerusalem on the 1st of Nissan in the 20th year of his reign (that is, March 5th, 444 BC; see *Nehemiah 2:1-8*). 173,880 days from March 5th 444 BC ends at March 30th 33 AD. Here's the math:

March 5th 444 BC to March 5th 33 AD = 476 years (1 B.C. to 1 A.D. is one year, there is no year zero). 476 x 365.24219879 days (which is the length of one year according to our modern calendar) = 173,855 days. March 5th to March 30th is another 25 days. 173,855 days + 25 days = 173,880 days.

March 30th, 33 AD was exactly 5 days before Passover on April 3rd, 33 AD. According to John's Gospel, the Triumphant Entry took place 5 days before Passover: *"Then, six days before the Passover, Jesus came to Bethany, where Lazarus was who had been dead, whom He had raised from the dead. ... Now a great many of the Jews knew that He was there; and they came, not for Jesus' sake only, but that they might also see Lazarus, whom He had raised from the dead. But the chief priests plotted to put Lazarus to death also, because on account of him many of the Jews went away and believed in Jesus. The next day a great multitude that had come to the feast, when they heard that Jesus was coming to Jerusalem, took branches of palm trees and went out to meet Him, and cried out: 'Hosanna! Blessed is He who comes in the name of the LORD! The King of Israel!'" (John 12:1, 9-13)*

The day after six days before the Passover equals five days before the Passover. March 30th was the Triumphal Entry, the day upon which Christ presented Himself to the nation of Israel as their Messiah, the first time in His entire ministry that He allowed Himself to be publicly proclaimed as the Messiah (*Matthew 21:8-16; Luke 19:37-40; cf. Matthew 16:13-20; Mark 8:27-30; 9:9 & 10; Luke 9:18-21; John 6:14 & 15*). He was crucified four days later, the day before Passover. Within one generation Titus razed Jerusalem and destroyed the temple.

Based on these points, we believe that Jesus' ministry lasted about three and a half years, from sometime around 29 AD until the spring of 33 AD.

∝

54. Question: "If Jesus was God, how could He pray to God? Was Jesus praying to Himself?"

To understand Jesus as God on earth praying to His Father who was God in heaven, we need to realize that the eternal Father and the eternal Son had an eternal relationship before Jesus took upon Himself humanity. Please read *John 5:19-27*, particularly *5:23* where Jesus teaches that the Father sent the Son (also read *John 15:10*). Jesus did not become the Son of God when He was born in Bethlehem many years ago. He has always been the Son of God from eternity past, still is, and always will be.

Isaiah 9:6 tells us that the Son was given and the child was born. Jesus was always a part of the Tri-unity relationship along with the Holy Spirit. The Tri-unity always existed, the Father God, the Son God, and the Spirit God. Not three Gods, but one God existing as three persons. Jesus taught that He and His Father were one (*John 10:30*). Jesus meant that He and His Father, and of course the Holy Spirit, were of the same substance, the same essence, God or deity. Three co-equal persons existing as God. These three had and continue to have an eternal relationship.

What happened when Jesus, the eternal Son of God, took upon Himself sinless humanity, is that He also took on the form of a servant, giving up His heavenly glory (*cf. Philippians 2:5-11*). As the God-man, He had to learn obedience (*Hebrews 5:8*) to His Father as He was tempted by Satan, accused falsely by men, rejected by His people, and eventually crucified. His praying to His heavenly Father was to ask for power (*John 11:41-42*) and wisdom (*Mark 1:35; 6:46*). His praying showed His dependence upon His Father in His humanity to carry out His Father's plan of redemption (note Christ's high priestly prayer in *John 17*) and then to ultimately submit to His Father's will in the Garden to go to the cross to pay the penalty for our breaking God's law, which is death (*Matthew 26:31-46*). Of course, He rose from the grave bodily, winning for us forgiveness and eternal life right now when we accept Him as personal Savior.

There is no problem with the Son as God praying or talking to the Father as God. As mentioned, they had an eternal relationship before Christ took upon Himself humanity. In His humanity, this relationship is depicted in the Gospels so we can see how the Son of God in His humanity carried out His Father's will so redemption could be won for all (*John 6:38*). Christ's continual submission to His heavenly Father was empowered and kept focused through His prayer life. Christ's example of prayer is left for us to follow.

Jesus Christ was no less God on earth when praying to God His Father in Heaven. He was depicting how even in sinless humanity it is necessary to have a vital prayer life to do His Father's will. Jesus' praying to the Father was a demonstration of His relationship, within the Trinity, with the Father and an example for us that we must rely on God, through prayer, for the strength and wisdom we need. Since Christ, as the God-man, needed to have a vibrant prayer life, so should the follower of Christ today!

$\propto$

55. Question: "Why did God send Jesus when He did? Why not earlier? Why not later?"

"But when the fullness of the time had come, God sent forth His Son, born of a woman, born under the law," (Galatians 4:4). The above verse declares that God the Father sent His Son when *"the fullness of time had come."* There were many things occurring at the time of the first century that, at least by human reasoning, seem to make it ideal for Christ to come then. These include the following:

⇒ There was a great anticipation that the Messiah would come among the Jews of that time. The Roman rule over Israel made the Jews hungry for the Messiah's coming.

⇒ Rome had unified much of the world under its government, giving a sense of unity to the various lands. Also, because the empire was relatively peaceful, travel was possible by the early Christians to spread the gospel that would not have been possible during other times.

⇒ While Rome had conquered militarily, Greece had conquered culturally. A "common" form of the Greek language (different from classical Greek) was the trade language and was spoken throughout the empire, making it possible to communicate the gospel to many different people groups through that one common language.

⇒ The fact that many people's idols had failed to give them victory over the Roman conquerors caused many to abandon their worship. At the same time in the more "cultured" cities, the Greek philosophy and science of the time left others spiritually empty in the same way that the atheism of Communist governments leaves a spiritual void today

⇒ The mystery religions of the time emphasized a savior-god and required worshipers to offer bloody sacrifices, thus making the gospel of Christ, involving one ultimate sacrifice, not unbelievable to them. The Greeks also believed in the immortality of the soul (but not of the body).

⇒ The Roman army recruited soldiers from among the provinces, introducing these men to Roman culture and to ideas (such as the gospel) that had not reached those outlying provinces yet. The earliest introduction of the gospel to Britain was the result of the efforts of Christian soldiers stationed there.

Again, the above statements are based on men looking at that time and their speculation why that particular point in history was a good time for Christ to come. But we understand that God's ways are above our ways and these may or may not have been some reasons for why He chose that particular time to send His Son. From the context of *Galatians 3 and 4*, it is evident that God sought to lay a foundation through the Jewish Law that would prepare for the coming of the Messiah. The Law was meant to help people understand the depth of their sinfulness (in that they were incapable in keeping the Law) so that they might more readily accept the cure for that sin in Jesus the Messiah (*Galatians 3:22-23; Romans 3:19-20*). The Law also served as a "tutor" (*Galatians 3:24*) to bring people to Jesus as the Messiah. It did this through its many prophecies concerning the Messiah which Jesus fulfilled. Add to this the sacrificial system that pointed to the need for a sacrifice for sin as well as its own temporary nature (with each sacrifice always requiring later additional ones). Old Testament history also painted pictures of the person and work of Christ through several events and religious feasts (such as the willingness of Abraham to offer up Isaac or the details of the Passover during the exodus from Egypt, etc.).

Lastly, Christ came when He did in fulfillment of specific prophecy. *Daniel 9:24-27* speaks of the "seventy 'weeks'" or the seventy "sevens." From the context, these "weeks" or "sevens" refer to groups of seven years, not seven days. We can examine history and line up the details of the first sixty-nine weeks (the seventieth week will take place at a future point). The countdown of the seventy weeks begins with *"the going forth of the command to restore and build Jerusalem" (verse 25)*. This command was given by Artaxerxes Longimanus in 445 B.C. (see *Nehemiah 2:5*). After 7 "sevens" plus 62 "sevens," or 69 x 7 years, it states that *"Messiah shall be cut off, but not for Himself and that the city and the sanctuary would be destroyed"* and that the *"end of it shall be with a flood"* (meaning major destruction) *(verse 26)*. Here we have an unmistakable reference to the Savior's death on the cross. A century ago in his book The Coming Prince, Sir Robert Anderson gave detailed calculations of the sixty-nine weeks, using 'prophetic years,' allowing for leap years, errors in the calendar, the change from B.C. to A.D., etc., and figured that the sixty-nine weeks ended on the very day of Jesus' triumphal entry into Jerusalem, five days before His death. Whether one uses this timetable or not, the point is that the timing of Christ's incarnation ties in with this detailed prophecy recorded by Daniel over five hundred years beforehand.

The timing of Christ's incarnation was such that the people of that time were prepared for His coming, and the people of every century since then have more than sufficient evidence that Jesus was indeed the promised Messiah through His fulfillment of the Scriptures that pictured and prophesied His coming in detail.

$\propto$

56. Question: "What is the meaning of those who were raised to life at Jesus' death (Matthew 27:52-53)?"

Matthew 27:50-53 records, "And Jesus cried out again with a loud voice, and yielded up His spirit. And behold, the veil of the temple was torn in two from top to bottom; and the earth shook and the rocks were split. The tombs were opened, and many bodies of the saints who had fallen asleep were raised; and coming out of the tombs after His resurrection they entered the holy city and appeared to many."

This event occurred as a testimony to the immortal power ascribed to Jesus Christ alone (*1 Timothy 6:14-16*). Only God has the power of life and death (*1 Samuel 2:6; Deuteronomy 32:29*). Therefore, the resurrection is the cornerstone of Christianity. All other religions and their respective leaders do not serve a risen Lord. By overcoming death, Jesus Christ immediately receives precedence because He came back to life when everyone else did not. The resurrection has given us a reason to tell others about Him and place trust in God (*1 Corinthians 15:14*). The resurrection has given us assurance that our sins are forgiven (*1 Corinthians 15:17*). Paul clearly says in this verse that no resurrection equals zero forgiveness of our sins. And, finally, the resurrection has given us a reason to have hope today (*1 Corinthians 15:20-28*). If Christ was not raised from the dead, then Christians would be no better off spiritually than non-Christians. But the fact is that God did raise *"Jesus our Lord from the dead, who was delivered up because of our offenses, and was raised because of our justification" (Romans 4:24 & 25)*.

The raising of the saints fits into the rhetorical devices and strategies used by Matthew in his gospel. Examining *Ezekiel 37* and the bones raised to life in connection with this story reveals that an Old Testament prophecy was fulfilled in the raising of these saints. Additionally, the raising of the saints relates directly to the coming kingdom. The raising of a few and not all of the saints shows that Jesus has power to resurrect, but also points forward to the second coming and judgment of Jesus Christ, which will include all those whose names are written in the Book Life by faith in the grace of God. Knowing that Jesus has died and conquered death through His resurrection ought to hasten our desire to repent and trust Him alone for salvation so we too can one day be resurrected *"in the twinkling of an eye" (1 Corinthians 15:52)*.

$\propto$

57. Question: "Was Jesus a pacifist?"

According to Webster's dictionary, a pacifist is someone who is opposed to violence, especially war, for any purpose, often accompanied by the refusal to bear arms by reason of conscience or religious conviction.

While Jesus is the *"prince of peace" (Isaiah 9:6)*, He was not, and is not, a pacifist. *Revelation 19:15*, speaking of Jesus declares, *"Out of His mouth comes a sharp sword with which to strike down the nations. He will rule them with an iron scepter. He treads the winepress of the fury of the wrath of God Almighty." Ecclesiastes 3:1, 3, & 8* say, *"There is a time for everything and a season for every activity under the heaven... a time to kill and a time to heal, a time to tear down and a time to build... a time to love and a time to hate, a time for war and a time for peace." Daniel 9:26* says that *"war will continue until the end, and desolations have been decreed." Matthew 24:6-8* says, *"You will hear of wars and rumors of wars, but see to it that you are not alarmed. Such things must happen, but the end is still to come. Nation will rise against nation, and kingdom against kingdom. There will be famines and earthquakes in various places. All these are the beginning of birth pains."*

Jesus Himself said, *"Do not suppose that I have come to bring peace to the earth. I did not come to bring peace, but a sword. For I have come to turn 'a man against his father, a daughter against her mother, a daughter-in-law against her mother-in-law---a man's enemies will be the members of his own household'" (Matthew 10:34-36). "From the days of John the Baptist until now, the kingdom of heaven has been forcefully advancing, and forceful men lay hold of it" (Matthew 11:12).*

We are commanded to hate what is evil and cling to what is good (*Romans 12:9*). In doing so we must take a stand against what is evil in this world and pursue righteousness (*2 Timothy 2:22*). Jesus did this and, in so doing, spoke openly against the religious and political rulers of His time because they were not seeking a righteousness from God, but rather of their own making (*Luke 20:1-2, Romans 9:31-33*). Zeal for God's righteousness consumed Jesus, and He was not afraid to stand up against those who opposed and dishonored His Father (*John 2:15-17*, see also *Numbers 25:11*). *"Those who hate Him He will repay to their face by destruction; He will not be slow to repay to their face those who hate Him" (Deuteronomy 7:10). "While people are saying, 'Peace and safety,' destruction will come on them suddenly, as labor pains on a pregnant woman, and they will not escape" (1 Thessalonians 5:3).*

The Old Testament is full of examples of how God used his people in war to bring judgment upon nations whose sin had reached its full measure (i.e. *Genesis 15:16, Numbers 21:3, 31:1-7, 32:20 & 21, Deuteronomy 7:1 & 2, Joshua 6:20 & 21, 8:1-8, 10:29-32, 11:7-20*). In raising the moral consciousness of the world, God must take the people as He finds them and introduce principles of righteousness within the moral framework with which the people can identify. We can be assured though, that it is always with justice that God judges and makes war (*Revelation 19:11*). *"For we know Him who said, 'It is mine to avenge; I will repay,' and again, 'The Lord will judge his people.' It is a dreadful thing to fall into the hands of the living God" (Hebrews 10:30 & 31).* What we can learn from these and other Biblical examples is that we are only to wage war when it is the will of God and not at our own discretion (*John 18:11, Numbers 14:41-45*). It is God's choice as to how and when He brings judgment of sin upon this world and its inhabitants, to display His holiness. We are simply called to follow Him (*Matthew 16:24 & 25*).

All of this may sound contradictory to the teachings of Jesus, God Himself, in which He instructs us to *"love your neighbor as yourself"* (*Matthew 19:19*), *"...turn the other cheek"* (*Matthew 5:39*), as well as the command, *"you shall not murder"* (*Exodus 20:13*). After all, we are told that God is love (*1 John 4:16*) and *"Blessed are the* peacemakers" (*Matthew 5:9*). The Bible also says in *2 Corinthians 10:4, "For though we live in the world, we do not wage war as the world does. The weapons we fight with are not weapons of the world. On the contrary, they have divine powers to demolish strongholds"* While all this is indeed true, it helps in examining these seemingly contradictory concepts from an eternal perspective, that we may gain a more complete understanding for Jesus' purpose in coming to this earth.

At the beginning of human history, God commanded mankind to rule over the earth (*Genesis 1:26-31; Hebrews 2:6-8*). When man disobeyed God, sin entered the world (Genesis 2:17, 3:6 & 7). By this one action, man sold his right to rule this world to Satan and at the same time became captive to sin himself (*John 8:34, 12:31; Romans 6:6; Ephesians 2:2, 6:12*). As a result, sinful men live in a world full of corruption, each person doing what is right in his own eyes, the whole time being led astray by their own evil desires (*Psalm 8:6, 51:5; Proverbs 14:12; Genesis 3:17; Romans 8:20, James 1:14 & 15*). It isn't hard to see that the whole world lies in Satan's power (*1 John 5:19*). Even Jesus did not dispute with him over the fact that he ruled the kingdoms of the world (*Matthew 4:8-10*). Therefore, there can be no lasting peace or restoration of the land until Jesus returns to redeem the land and man (*Galatians 4:4 & 5*).

Jesus came in the likeness of mankind, while still retaining his full authority as God, in order that He might redeem men from their sentence of death, and re-establish, for the believer, man's authority to rule (*Philippians 2:6-8, 1 Corinthians 15:21 & 22, 54-57, Revelation 20:6*). When Jesus died on the cross, He purchased back the land and men's souls from the dominion of Satan through the shedding of His own blood, the purchase price for redemption of man's sin (*Hebrews 9:22, Acts 20:28, 1 Peter 1:18 & 19, 1 Corinthians 6:20*). A day is coming, after severe judgment upon the earth, when Jesus will break the seal of the deed and end Satan's rule (*Revelation 5:1-10, 6-18, 19:11-21*). At the end of Jesus' 1,000 year reign upon this earth, Satan will be set free for a short time and war once again will be waged (*Revelation 20:7-10*). It is only at the end of that war, once the murderer of man, Satan, is destroyed by Jesus and His servants' blood is finally avenged, that wars will cease and peace will once again be established in the new heaven and new earth (*John 8:44, Deuteronomy 32:43, Daniel 7:13 & 14, 2 Peter 3:3-13, Revelation 21:1-4*). Until that time we are called to fight the good fight and keep the faith (*2 Timothy 4:7*).

58. Question: "After His resurrection, why did Jesus tell Mary not to touch Him, but later tell Thomas to touch Him?"

Jesus tells Mary, *"Touch Me not"* (*John 20:17*, KJV); but then later, speaking to Thomas, He says, *"Reach hither thy finger and behold My hands; and reach hither thy hand, and thrust it into My side" (verse 27)*. The seeming incongruity of Jesus' statements is resolved when we examine the language Jesus employed and consider the basic difference between the two situations.

In *John 20:17*, the word translated "touch" is a Greek word which means "to cling to, to lay hold of." This wasn't just a touch; it was a grip. Obviously, when Mary recognized Jesus, she immediately clung to Him. *Matthew 28:9* records the other women doing the same thing when they saw the resurrected Christ.

Mary's reaction was motivated, possibly, by several things. One is simply her loving devotion to the Lord. Mary is overwhelmed by the events of the morning, and as her grief turns to joy, she naturally embraces Jesus. Another motivation is Mary's desire to restore the fellowship that death had broken. She had lost Him once, and she was going to make sure she didn't lose Him again, she wanted to keep Jesus with her always. Also, Mary may have been thinking that this was the fulfillment of Jesus' promise to return (*John 14:3*), in which case He would take her (*and all believers*) with Him to heaven.

However, it was not Jesus' plan to stay in this world always, and His resurrection was not to be seen as His promised return. That is why He tells Mary of the ascension. His plan was to ascend to the Father and then send the Holy Spirit (*John 16:7; 20:22; Acts 2:1-4*). Fellowship with Jesus would continue, but it would be a spiritual communion, not a physical presence

In loosening Mary's hold on Him, Jesus was, in effect, saying this: "I know you desire to keep Me here, always present with you. I know you want everything to be just the same as before I died. But our relationship is about to change. I'm going to heaven, and you will have the Comforter in My place. You need to start walking by faith, Mary, not by sight."

When Jesus spoke to Thomas, it was not to counter a misplaced desire but to rebuke a lack of faith. Thomas had said he would not believe until he had touched the living body of Jesus (*John 20:25*). Jesus, knowing all about Thomas's declaration, offered His body as living proof of His resurrection. This was something He did on another occasion as well (*Luke 24:39-40*).

So, both Mary and Thomas needed more faith. Mary needed faith enough to let Jesus go. Thomas needed faith enough to believe without empirical proof. Mary needed to loosen her grip; Thomas needed to strengthen his. The resurrected Christ gave both of them the faith they needed.

$$\propto$$

59. Question: "What does it mean that Jesus is the 'first-born' over Creation?"

In a letter to the church at Colossae, the Apostle Paul gave an intriguing description of Jesus. In it, he explained Christ's relationship to God the Father and to creation. Some have claimed that Paul's description of Christ as the first-born of creation means that Jesus was created -- not eternal, not God. Such a doctrine, however, conflicts with the rest of the Bible. Christ could not be both Creator and created; *John 1* clearly names Him Creator. Let's take a careful look at the passage where Jesus is called the first-born.

Colossians 1:15-21 *"And He is the image of the invisible God, the first -born of all creation. For by Him all things were created, both in the heavens and on earth, visible and invisible, whether thrones or dominions or rulers or authorities all things have been created by Him and for Him. And He is before all things, and in Him all things hold together. He is also head of the body, the church; and He is the beginning, the first-born from the dead; so that He Himself might come to have first place in everything. For it was the Father's good pleasure for all the fullness to dwell in Him, and through Him to reconcile all things to Himself, having made peace through the blood of His cross; through Him, I say, whether things on earth or things in heaven."*

⇒ **Jesus is God** Christ's relationship to His Father begins with the phrase "the image of the invisible God." The word "image," meaning copy or likeness, expresses Christ's deity. This word involves more than a resemblance, more than a representation. He is God! Although He took on human form, He has the exact nature of His Father (*Hebrews 1:3*). The "Word" of *John 1:1* is a divine Person, not a philosophical abstraction. In the incarnation, the invisible God became visible in Christ; deity was clothed with humanity *(Matthew 17:2)*. God is in Christ: visible, audible, approachable, knowable, and available. All that God is, Christ is.

⇒ **Jesus is Lord of Creation** The description "first-born of all creation" speaks of Christ's preexistence. He is not a creature but the eternal Creator *(John 1:10)*. God created the world through Christ and redeemed the world through Christ *(Hebrews 1:2-4)*. Note that Jesus is called the first-born, not the first-created. The word "first-born" (Greek word "prototokos") signifies priority. In the culture of the Ancient Near East, the first-born was not necessarily the oldest child. First-born referred not to birth order but to rank. The first-born possessed the inheritance and leadership.

Therefore, the phrase expresses Christ's sovereignty over creation. After resurrecting Jesus from the dead, God gave Him authority over the Earth *(Matthew 28:18)*. Jesus created the world, saved the world, and rules the world. He is the self-existent, acknowledged Head of creation. The phrase recognizes Him as the Messiah: *"I will make Him [Christ] My first-born, higher than the kings of the earth" (Psalm 89:27)*.

Six times the Lord Jesus is declared to be the first-born of God (see *Romans 8:29; Colossians 1:15, 18; Hebrews 1:6; 12:23; Revelation 1:5*). These passages declare the preexistence, the sovereignty, and the redemption that Christ offers.

Thus, the phrase "first-born of all creation" proclaims Christ's preeminence. As the eternal Son of God, He created the universe. He is the Ruler of creation!

60. Question: "How is Jesus different from other religious leaders?"

In a sense asking this question is sort of like asking how the sun differs from other stars in our solar system, the point being that there are no other stars in our solar system!

The point is that no other "religious leader" even compares to Jesus Christ. Every other religious leader is either alive or dead. Jesus Christ is the only one who was dead (He died in our place, for our sins, according *I Corinthians 15:1-8*) and is now alive. Indeed, He proclaims in *Revelation 1:17 & 18* that He is alive forevermore! No other religious leader even makes such a claim, a claim that is either true or utterly preposterous.

Another important difference is found in the very nature of Christianity. The essence of Christianity is Christ. Crucified, resurrected, ascended into Heaven, returning someday. Without Him, and without His resurrection, there is no Christianity. Compare that with other major religions. Hinduism, for example, can stand or fall entirely apart from any of the "great Swamis" who founded it. Buddhism is the same story. Even Islam is based upon the sayings and teachings of Mohammed, not upon the claim that he came back to life from the dead.

The Apostle Paul, in *1 Corinthians 15:13-19*, says that if Christ was not raised from the dead, then our faith is empty and we are still in our sins! What he is saying is that the truth claims of Christianity are based simply and solely upon the resurrected Jesus Christ! If He did not, in fact, come back from the dead, in time and space, then there is no truth to Christianity whatsoever. Over and over again throughout the New Testament the apostles and evangelists base the truth of the Gospel upon the Resurrection.

One other significant point that we dare not overlook is the exceedingly important fact that Jesus Christ claimed to be the "Son of God" (a Hebraism meaning "characterized by God") as well as the "Son of Man" (a Hebraism meaning "characterized by Man"). In many varied passages, He makes claims to be equal with the Father (see, for example, *John 10:29-33*). To Him are ascribed all of the prerogatives and attributes of Deity. Yet He was also a man, born of a virgin (*Matthew 1:18-25; Luke 1:26-56*). Having lived a sinless life, He was crucified in order to pay for the sins of all men: *"He Himself is the satisfaction of*

God's wrath for our sins; and not for ours only, but for those of the whole world" (1 John 2:2), and then He was resurrected from the dead three days later. He is fully God and fully Man, the "theanthropos" [from the Greek for God (theos) - Man (anthropos)]; yet He is one person.

The very Person and Work of Christ poses for us a question that we cannot avoid: What will you do with Jesus? We cannot simply dismiss Him. We cannot ignore Him. He is the central figure in all of human history, and if He died for the sins of the whole world, then He died for yours as well. The Apostle Peter tells us in *Acts 4:12, "And there is salvation in no one else; for there is no other name under heaven that has been given among men by which we must be saved."* If we believe on the Lord Jesus Christ as our Savior from sin, we will be saved.

$\propto\!\!\prec$

61. Question: "Is 'virgin' or 'young woman' the correct translation of Isaiah 7:14?"

Isaiah 7:14 reads, *"Therefore the Lord himself will give you a sign: the virgin will be with child and will give birth to a son, and will call him Immanuel."* Quoting *Isaiah 7:14, Matthew 1:23* reads, *"The virgin will be with child and will give birth to a son, and they will call him Immanuel, which means, 'God with us.'"* Christians point to this "virgin birth" as evidence of Messianic prophecy fulfilled by Jesus. Is this a valid example of fulfilled prophecy? Is *Isaiah 7:14* predicting the virgin birth of Jesus? Is "virgin" even the proper translation of the Hebrew word used in *Isaiah 7:14?*

The Hebrew word in *Isaiah 7:14* is "almah" and its inherent meaning is "young woman." "Almah" can mean "virgin," as young unmarried women in ancient Hebrew culture were assumed to be virgins. Again, though, the word does not necessarily imply virginity. "Almah" occurs seven times in the Hebrew Scriptures (*Genesis 24:43; Exodus 2:8; Psalm 68:25; Proverbs 30:19; Song of Solomon 1:3; 6:8; Isaiah 7:14*). None of these instances demands the meaning "virgin," but neither do they deny the possible meaning of "virgin." There is no conclusive argument for "almah" in *Isaiah 7:14* being either "young woman" or "virgin." However, it is interesting to note, that in the 3rd century B.C., when a panel of Hebrew scholars and Jewish rabbis began the process of translating the Hebrew Scriptures into Greek, they used the specific Greek word for virgin, "parthenos," not the more generic Greek word for "young woman." The Septuagint translators, 200+ years before the birth of Christ, and with no inherent belief in a "virgin birth," translated "almah" in *Isaiah 7:14* as "virgin," not "young woman." This gives evidence that "virgin" is a possible, even likely, meaning of the term.

With all that said, even if the meaning "virgin" is ascribed to "almah" in *Isaiah 7:14*, does that make *Isaiah 7:14* a Messianic prophecy about Jesus, as *Matthew 1:23* claims? In the context of *Isaiah chapter 7*, the Aramites and Israelites were seeking to conquer Jerusalem, and King Ahaz was fearful. The Prophet Isaiah approaches King Ahaz and declares that Aram and Israel would not be successful in conquering Jerusalem (*verses 7-9*). The Lord offers Ahaz the opportunity to receive a sign (*verse 10*), but Ahaz refuses to put God to the test (*verse 11*). God responds by giving the sign Ahaz should look for, "the virgin will be with child and will give birth to a son...but before the boy knows enough to reject the wrong and choose the right, the land of the two kings you dread will be laid waste." In this prophecy, God is essentially saying that within a few years' time, Israel and Aram will be destroyed. At first glance, *Isaiah 7:14* has no connection with a promised virgin birth of the Messiah. However, the Apostle Matthew, writing under the inspiration of the Holy Spirit, connects the virgin birth of Jesus (*Matthew 1:23*) with the prophecy in *Isaiah 7:14*. Therefore, *Isaiah 7:14* should be understood as being a "double prophecy," referring primarily to the situation King Ahaz was facing, but secondarily to the coming Messiah who would be the ultimate deliverer.

62. Question: "Why did blood and water come out of Jesus' side when He was pierced?"

The Roman flogging or scourging that Jesus endured prior to being crucified normally consisted of 39 lashes, but could have been more (Mark 15:15; John 19:1). The whip that was used, called a flagrum, consisted of braided leather thongs with metal balls and pieces of sharp bone woven into or intertwined with the braids. The balls added weight to the whip, causing deep bruising and contusions as the victim was struck. The pieces of bone served to cut into the flesh. As the beating continued, the resulting cuts were so severe that the skeletal muscles, underlying veins, sinews, and bowels of victims were exposed. This beating was so severe that at times victims would not survive it in order to go on to be crucified.

Those who were flogged would often go into hypovolemic shock, a term that refers to low blood volume. In other words, the person would have lost so much blood he would go into shock. The results of this would be:

1) The heart would race to pump blood that was not there.
2) The victim would collapse or faint due to low blood pressure.
3) The kidneys would shut down to preserve body fluids.
4) The person would experience extreme thirst as the body desired to replenish lost fluids.

There is evidence from Scripture that Jesus experienced hypovolemic shock as a result of being flogged. As Jesus carried His own cross to Golgotha (*John 19:17*), He collapsed, and a man named Simon was forced to either carry the cross or help Jesus carry the cross the rest of way to the hill (*Matthew 27:32 & 33; Mark 15:21 & 22; Luke 23:26*). This collapse indicates Jesus had low blood pressure. Another indicator that Jesus suffered from hypovolemic shock was that He declared He was thirsty as He hung on the cross (*John 19:28*), indicating His body's desire to replenish fluids.

Prior to death, the sustained rapid heartbeat caused by hypovolemic shock also causes fluid to gather in the sack around the heart and around the lungs. This gathering of fluid in the membrane around the heart is called pericardial effusion, and the fluid gathering around the lungs is called pleural effusion. This explains why, after Jesus died and a Roman soldier thrust a spear through Jesus' side (probably His right side, piercing both the lungs and the heart), blood and water came from His side just as John recorded in his Gospel (John 19:34).

><

63. Question: "What is the meaning and importance of the ascension of Jesus Christ?"

After Jesus rose from the dead, He *"presented Himself alive"* (*Acts 1:3*) to the women near the tomb (*Matthew 28:9-10*), to His disciples (*Luke 24:36-43*), and to more than 500 others (*1 Corinthians 15:6*). In the days following His resurrection, Jesus taught His disciples about the kingdom of God (*Acts 1:3*).

Forty days after the resurrection, Jesus and His disciples went to Mount Olivet, near Jerusalem. There, Jesus promised His followers that they would soon receive the Holy Spirit, and He instructed them to remain in Jerusalem until the Spirit had come. Then Jesus blessed them, and as He gave the blessing, He began to ascend into heaven. The account of Jesus' ascension is found in *Luke 24:50 & 51* and *Acts 1:9-11*.

It is plain from Scripture that Jesus' ascension was a literal, bodily return to heaven. He rose from the ground gradually and visibly, observed by many intent onlookers. As the disciples strained to catch a last glimpse of Jesus, a cloud hid Him from their view, and two angels appeared and promised Christ's return *"in just the same way that you have watched Him go" (Acts 1:11)*. The Ascension of Jesus Christ is meaningful for several reasons:

⇒ It signaled the end of His earthly ministry. God the Father had lovingly sent His Son into the world at Bethlehem, and now the Son was returning to the Father. The period of human limitation was at an end.

⇒ It signified success in His earthly work. All that He had come to do, He had accomplished.

⇒ It marked the return of His heavenly glory. Jesus' glory had been veiled during His sojourn on earth, with one brief exception at the Transfiguration (*Matthew 17:1-9*).

⇒ It symbolized His exaltation by the Father (*Ephesians 1:20-23*). The One with whom the Father is well pleased (*Matthew 17:5*) was received up in honor and given a name above all names (*Philippians 2:9*).

⇒ It allowed Him to prepare a place for us (*John 14:2*).

⇒ It indicated the beginning of His new work as High Priest (*Hebrews 4:14-16*) and Mediator of the New Covenant

(*Hebrews 9:15*).

⇒ It set the pattern for His return. When Jesus comes to set up the Kingdom, He will return just as He left-literally, bodily, and visibly in the clouds (*Acts 1:11; Daniel 7:13-14; Matthew 24:30; Revelation 1:7*).

Currently, the Lord Jesus is in heaven. The Scriptures frequently picture Him at the right hand of the Father-a position of honor and authority (*Psalm 110:1; Ephesians 1:20; Hebrews 8:1*). Christ is the Head of the Church (*Colossians 1:18*), the giver of spiritual gifts (*Ephesians 4:7 & 8*), and the One who fills all in all (*Ephesians 4:9 & 10*).

⊂✕

64. Question: "Can the various resurrection accounts from the four Gospels be harmonized?"

The events surrounding Jesus' resurrection can be difficult to piece together. We must remember two things: first, the news of Jesus' resurrection produced much excitement in Jerusalem, and in the ensuing chaos many people were going many different directions. Groups were separated, and several different groups paid visits to the tomb, possibly more than once. Second, the writers of the Gospels did not attempt an exhaustive narrative; in other words, Matthew, Mark, Luke, and John had no intention of telling us every detail of the resurrection or every event in the order that it happened.

In the battle with skeptics regarding Jesus' resurrection, Christians are in a "no-win" situation. If the resurrection accounts harmonize perfectly, skeptics will claim that the writers of the Gospels conspired together. If the resurrection accounts have some differences, skeptics will claim that the Gospels contradict each other and therefore cannot be trusted. It is our contention that the resurrection accounts can be harmonized and do not contradict each other.

However, even if the resurrection accounts cannot be perfectly harmonized, that does not make them untrustworthy. By any reasonable evaluation, the resurrection accounts from the four Gospels are superbly consistent eyewitness testimonies. The central truths - that Jesus was resurrected from the dead and that the resurrected Jesus appeared to many people - are clearly taught in each of the four Gospels. The apparent inconsistencies are in "side issues." How many angels did they see in the tomb, one or two? (Perhaps one person only saw one angel, while the other person saw two angels.) To how many women did Jesus appear, and to whom did He appear first? (While each Gospel has a slightly different sequence to the appearances, none of them claims to be giving the precise chronological order.) So, while the resurrection accounts may seem to be inconsistent, it cannot be proven that the accounts are contradictory.

Here is a possible harmony of the narratives of the resurrection of Christ and His post-resurrection appearances, in chronological order:

⇒ Jesus is buried, as several women watch (*Matthew 27:57-61; Mark 15:42-47; Luke 23:50-56; John 19:38-42*).

⇒ The tomb is sealed and a guard is set (*Matthew 27:62-66*).

⇒ At least 3 women, including Mary Magdalene, Mary the mother of James, and Salome, prepare spices to go to the tomb (*Matthew 28:1; Mark 16:1*).

⇒ An angel descends from heaven, rolls the stone away, and sits on it. There is an earthquake, and the guards faint (*Matthew 28:2-4*).

⇒ The women arrive at the tomb and find it empty. Mary Magdalene leaves the other women there and runs to tell the disciples (*John 20:1 & 2*).

⇒ The women still at the tomb see two angels who tell them that Jesus is risen and who instruct them to tell the disciples to go to Galilee (*Matthew 28:5-7; Mark 16:2-8; Luke 24:1-8*).

⇒ The women leave to bring the news to the disciples (*Matthew 28:8*).

⇒ The guards, having roused themselves, report the empty tomb to the authorities, who bribe the guards to say the body was stolen (*Matthew 28:11-15*).

⇒ Mary the mother of James and the other women, on their way to find the disciples, see Jesus (*Matthew 28:9 & 10*).

⇒ The women relate what they have seen and heard to the disciples (*Luke 24:9-11*).

⇒ Peter and John run to the tomb, see that it is empty, and find the grave clothes (*Luke 24:12; John 20:2-10*).

⇒ Mary Magdalene returns to the tomb. She sees the angels, and then she sees Jesus (*John 20:11-18*).

⇒ Later the same day, Jesus appears to Peter (*Luke 24:34; 1 Corinthians 15:5*).

⇒ Still on the same day, Jesus appears to Cleopas and another disciple on their way to Emmaus (*Luke 24:13:32*).

⇒ That evening, the two disciples report the event to the Eleven in Jerusalem (*Luke 24:32-35*).

⇒ Jesus appears to ten disciples, Thomas is missing (*Luke 24:36 -43; John 20:19-25*).

⇒ Jesus appears to all eleven disciples, Thomas included (*John 20:26-31*).

⇒ Jesus appears to seven disciples by the Sea of Galilee (*John 21:1-25*).

⇒ Jesus appears to about 500 disciples in Galilee (*1 Corinthians 15:6*).

⇒ Jesus appears to His half-brother James (*1 Corinthians 15:7*).

⇒ Jesus commissions His disciples (*Matthew 28:16-20*).

⇒ Jesus teaches His disciples the Scriptures and promises to send the Holy Spirit (*Luke 24:44-49; Acts 1:4 & 5*).

⇒ Jesus ascends into heaven (*Luke 24:50-53; Acts 1:6-12*).

∝

65. Question: "What does it mean that Jesus is God's only begotten son?"

The phrase "only begotten Son" occurs in *John 3:16*, which reads in the King James Version as, "For God so loved the world, that He gave His only begotten Son, that whosoever believeth in Him should not perish, but have everlasting life." The phrase "only begotten" translates the Greek word monogenes. This word is variously translated into English as "only," "one and only," and "only begotten."

It's this last phrase ("only begotten" used in the KJV, NASB and the NKJV) that causes problems. False teachers have latched onto this phrase to try to prove their false teaching that Jesus Christ isn't God; i.e., that Jesus isn't equal in essence to God as the Second Person of the Trinity. They see the word "begotten" and say that Jesus is a created being because only someone who had a beginning in time can be "begotten." What this fails to note is that "begotten" is an English translation of a Greek word. As such, we have to look at the original meaning of the Greek word, not transfer English meanings into the text.

So what does monogenes mean? According to the Greek-English Lexicon of the New Testament and Other Early Christian Literature (BAGD, 3rd Edition), monogenes has two primary definitions. The first definition is "pertaining to being the only one of its kind within a specific relationship." This is the meaning attached to its use in *Hebrews 11:17* when the writer refers to Isaac as Abraham's "only begotten son." Abraham had more than one son, but Isaac was the only son he had by Sarah and the only son of the covenant.

The second definition is "pertaining to being the only one of its kind or class, unique in kind." This is the meaning that is implied in *John 3:16*. In fact, John is the only New Testament writer who uses this word in reference to Jesus (see John *1:14, 18; 3:16, 18; 1 John 4:9*). John was primarily concerned with demonstrating that Jesus was the Son of God (*John 20:31*), and he uses this word to highlight Jesus as uniquely God's Son, sharing the same divine nature as God, as opposed to believers who are God's sons and daughters through faith.

The bottom line is that terms such as "Father" and "Son," that are descriptive of God and Jesus, are human terms used to help us understand the relationship between the different Persons of the Trinity. If you can understand the relationship between a human father and a human son, then you can understand, in part, the relationship between the First and Second Persons of the Trinity. The analogy breaks down if you try to take it too far and teach, as some Christian cults (such as the Jehovah's Witnesses), that Jesus was literally "begotten" as in "produced" or "created" by God the Father.

66. Question: "Is the rock opera *Jesus Christ Superstar* biblical?"

The rock opera *Jesus Christ Superstar* by Andrew Lloyd Webber and

Tim Rice and the movie of the same name, directed by Norman Jewison, tell the story of the final days of Jesus. The opera's theme deals with fame and how popularity can deceive and corrupt.

Superficially at least, *Jesus Christ Superstar* contains many elements of the biblical narrative: Jesus has disciples, and He teaches. The priests Caiaphas and Annas, out of jealousy and fear, foment a plot to destroy Jesus. Mary Magdalene and other women serve Him. Judas plans to betray Him. Jesus enters Jerusalem amid celebration, cleanses the temple, and eats a meal with His disciples. After He prays in a garden, He is arrested, taken before several officials, and beaten. Peter denies knowing the Lord, and Judas hangs himself. Jesus is crucified. None of this conflicts with the biblical record.

Upon closer inspection, however, the biblical failings of *Jesus Christ Superstar* become apparent. Any time a story is retold, a certain amount of interpretation is required. The author's ideas, presuppositions, and opinions are injected. In this retelling of Jesus' passion, the character and motivations of both Jesus and Judas are re-imagined and reinterpreted.

Judas has the first song. In it, he complains about the fact that Jesus has been caught up in His own fame and rages over the fact that Jesus won't listen to him. Judas calls Jesus' followers "blind," accuses them of twisting Jesus' words, and expresses a desire to "strip away the myth from the man." Considering these words come from Judas, we might be prone to dismiss them as a villain's distortion. However, the insistence that Jesus is "just a man" is repeated later by Mary Magdalene in one of the opera's most famous songs, "I Don't Know How to Love Him."

In the next scene, Judas objects to Mary's proximity to Jesus. He warns Jesus of the scandal that will erupt if Jesus is not more careful. Later, when Mary anoints Jesus, Judas objects again, reminding Jesus that their mission is to the poor. Jesus' response is for Judas to "enjoy the good" while he has it. Throughout this scene, we have the contrast of Mary's telling Jesus to "close your eyes," versus Judas's trying to open His eyes to the needs of society; as Mary sings, "Relax," Judas urges action on behalf of the poor. No mention is made of Judas's greed and thievery (*John 12:6*).

When Jesus enters Jerusalem, there is a celebration of His being a "superstar." Interestingly, there is no donkey; Jesus walks until He is lifted up above the crowd on a pallet. Also, unlike the biblical account, the praise is not quite spontaneous. Jesus initiates the singing at one point, and He even commands the crowd to "sing me your songs." He briefly teaches about the Kingdom of God saying, "You can win it."

The next scene has Jesus surrounded by adoring multitudes. There is a mention of salvation and a belief in God as the crowd offers Him their devotion and a kingdom. Judas looks on in disgust and disbelief. Jesus ends the celebration by speaking of death, which He says can only be conquered by dying. There is no mention of Jesus as the Life and no prediction of His resurrection.

In a later scene, Jesus is surrounded by people who need healing. No one is healed; rather, an overwhelmed Jesus cries out, "There's too many of you. There's too little of me. Leave me alone!"

When Judas meets with the Jewish council to betray Jesus, he makes it clear that he is only trying to "save" Jesus, who has let His own popularity spiral out of control. He takes the money they offer him unwillingly.

During the Last Supper, the disciples dream of lasting fame. Jesus bitterly accuses His disciples about not caring about Him: "For all you care, this wine could be my blood! For all you care, this bread could be my body!" He tells them to remember Him when they eat, but then He says, "I must be mad, thinking you'll remember me!" Judas leaves to complete the betrayal, because Jesus tells him he must.

Jesus' prayer in the garden is very telling. He admits that He has changed, that He is no longer inspired. Now He's only "sad and tired." After three years of trying to serve God, Jesus has lost His original vision. Considering becoming a martyr, Jesus selfishly asks, "Will I be more noticed? What will be my reward?" This is in contrast to Judas's not wanting a reward for his betrayal. At the end of the prayer, Jesus finally submits to God's plan, sort of. The song ends with an equivocation: "Take me now, before I change my mind."

When Jesus is arrested, His disciples talk of fighting for Him. Jesus rebukes them with these words: "Stick to fishing from now on." This is as close to the Great Commission as the opera ever gets.

Pilate repeatedly calls Jesus "Someone Christ," a name which empha-sizes the fact that Jesus is a nobody, a fact which Jesus is desperately attempting to change through His martyrdom. Through the various trials, Judas keeps close by, wanting to see what will happen. Judas then returns the money to the priests, again expressing his wish to "save" Jesus.

In Pilate's second interview with Jesus, he asks Jesus if He is a king. Jesus' answer is fuzzy at best: "I have no kingdom. In this world, I'm through. There may be a kingdom for me somewhere, if you only knew" (see *John 18:36 & 37* for Jesus' real answer). When the mob cries out for His crucifixion, Pilate delivers a series of accusations against Jesus: "He's mad, ought to be locked up . . . he's a sad little man, not a king or god . . . he's misguided, thinks he's important . . . a misguided martyr . . . a misguided puppet." (What Pilate actually said was, *"I find no basis for a charge against him" [John 18:38].*)

After Jesus is whipped, the music immediately (and significantly) shifts into the "Superstar" theme. This is a way of saying that the mar-tyrdom has begun, and Jesus has won His fame. This idea is stressed in Judas's final song, in which he mentions both Buddha and Mohammed but says that Jesus has more appeal because of how He died. The opera ends with Jesus' crucifixion. There is no resurrection.

To summarize the theme of *Jesus Christ Superstar*, Jesus was not di-vine but was a fascinating and magnetic man of good intentions who let things get out of control. Overwhelmed by His own fame, He de-sired to return to a simpler, more sincere life, but He couldn't. Of the disciples, only Judas recognized what was happening. He hated what Jesus had become but still loved Him and wanted to help Him. Jesus saw only one way out of His predicament: to die as a martyr; then, per-haps, some of His good teaching might be remembered. For this, He needed Judas's help, and Judas agreed to sacrifice himself in order to "save" Jesus and His message.

Of course, this is not biblical. Jesus is more than just a man; He is the Son of God (*John 10:30*). Jesus never lost sight of His mission to seek and save the lost (*Luke 19:10*), which required His sacrificial death on the cross as payment for our sin (*1 Peter 3:18*). Jesus did not just die; He rose again (*1 Peter 1:3*).

Jesus Christ Superstar is more than a popular opera that happens to get some facts wrong. It is an attempt to rewrite history. It makes the trai-tor Judas Iscariot the hero and reduces the Lord Jesus Christ to a burnt-out celebrity who is in over His head.